영어회화
100일의
기적 2

영어회화 100일의 기적 2

지은이 문성현
펴낸이 임상진
펴낸곳 (주)넥서스

초판 1쇄 발행 2020년 12월 15일
초판 15쇄 발행 2024년 4월 5일

출판신고 1992년 4월 3일 제311-2002-2호
주소 10880 경기도 파주시 지목로 5
전화 (02)330-5500 팩스 (02)330-5555

ISBN 979-11-91209-01-3 13740

www.nexusbook.com

일상생활 표현으로 **진짜 영어를 말한다!**

영어회화 100일의 기적 2

문성현 지음

넥서스

100일의 기적을 위한 다짐!

나 _____는
영어회화 100일의 기적 2로
100일 뒤 반드시
영어 울렁증을 극복할 것이다.

영어회화가 어려우시죠?
이렇게 해 보세요.

독자 여러분, 안녕하세요. 직장 생활을 하며 독학한 내용을 공유하고자 출간한 책이 50만 부가 넘게 판매되어 벌써 6번째 책이 나오게 되었습니다. 저는 「영어회화 100일의 기적」이 많은 사랑을 받은 이유가 평범한 저의 일상을 영어로 표현했기 때문이라고 생각합니다.

지난 20년간 제가 영어 공부를 하면서 느낀 점은 대부분의 학습자들이 목표 설정을 하는 것과 이를 실행하는 방법에 문제가 있다는 것입니다. 영어권 국가에 살지 않으면서도 원어민 실력을 목표로 하거나 우리에게 필요한 표현이 아닌 원어민이 쓰는 표현을 무작정 습득하려고 하는 것은 영어 실력 향상에 도움이 되지 않습니다. 한국에 살고 있는 우리에게 필요한 영어는 지극히 한정되어 있습니다.

배운 영어 문장이 기억나지 않는 이유는 반복적인 활용을 통해 뇌에 각인이 되지 않았기 때문입니다. 즉, 매일 듣고 말하는 영어 문장만 머릿속에 남게 되는 것입니다. 우리 뇌는 가장 최근에 입력된 정보만 저장하도록 설계되어 있습니다. 그 말은 매일 반복해서 듣거나 말하지 않으면 내 것이 되기 어렵다는 뜻입니다. 따라서 효율적으로 영어 실력을 향상시키기 위해서는 우선 반복되는 일상에서 사용하는 표현부터 익히는 전략이 필요합니다.

이 책은 한국인이 일상생활에서 자주 접하는 100가지 상황을 설정하여 100일간 700개 이상의 표현을 배우고 미니 대화문으로 활용 능력을 높일 수 있도록 구성하였습니다. 한국어로 자주 사용하는 문장을 영어식 표현으로 바꾸어 연습하면 원어민과 대화가 한층 원활해질 것입니다. 또한, 여러분의 자발적인 학습에 도움을 드리고자 팟캐스트와 유튜브 채널을 통해 해설 강의와 복습 영상을 꾸준히 제공할 예정입니다.

100일간의 도전을 통해 여러분의 영어 실력에 의미 있는 변화가 있기를 진심으로 고대합니다.

저자 **문성현**

기적의 100일 학습법

DAY 001~005

MP3와 저자 강의를 들어 보세요

〈영어회화 100일의 기적 2〉
전용 **모바일 페이지**를 통해
MP3와 저자 강의 듣기

· 녹음 강의
· 동영상 강의

① 우리 일상생활에서 엄선한
오늘의 표현

Day 001

MP3 강의 듣기

② 원어민이 직접 녹음한
MP3와 저자의 녹음 강의로
학습 효과 증대

DAY 001

봄꽃 나들이

Day 001

MP3 강의 듣기

What do you like about spring?

봄이 되면 뭐가 좋아?

A What do you like about spring?
B A lot of trees burst into blossom* all across the country*.
A Let's check out the cherry blossom festival* tomorrow.
B Sure. We have to leave early to beat the traffic.
A I'll call you first thing in the morning*.
B I'll pack a big lunch for us.

A 넌 봄이 되면 뭐가 좋아?
B 전국적으로 나무에 꽃이 만개하잖아.
A 내일 벚꽃 축제에 같이 가자.
B 좋아. 벚꽃 출발해서 교통 혼잡을 피하자.
A 아침 일어나자마자 바로 전화할게.
B 도시락 많이 싸 올게.

이 내표현 체크

· burst into blossom (꽃이 만개하다) · all across the country 전국적으로
· cherry blossom festival 벚꽃 축제 · first thing in the morning 일어나자마자 / 출근하자마자

16

Mini Dialogues

❶ **What do you like about sth/sb?**
~에 대해 뭐가 좋아?
A What do you like about your boyfriend?
B He has a warm heart and a nice voice.
A 남자 친구 어디가 좋아?
B 마음이 따뜻하고 목소리가 좋아.

❷ **check out sth** ~를 보러 가다 / 가 보다
A Have you been to the new kids café nearby?
B Yes. That's cool. You should go and check it out.
A 근처에 새로 오픈한 키즈 카페 가 본 적 있어?
B 그럼. 정말 좋더라. 너도 꼭 한번 가 봐.

❸ **beat the traffic** 교통 혼잡을 피하다
A I should leave now. I want to beat the traffic.
B Oh, it's already past 5. You'd better hurry.
A 난 이제 가 봐야 돼. 차 막히기 전에 가려고.
B 아, 벌써 5시가 지났구나. 어서 서둘러.

❹ **pack a (big) lunch** 도시락을 (많이) 싸다
A I'm looking forward to our picnic tomorrow.
B So am I. Don't forget to pack a lunch.
A 어떤 주말에 가는 피크닉 기대돼고 있어.
B 나도. 그래. 도시락 싸 오는 거 잊지 마.

Mini Dialogues

❶ **What do you like about sth**
~에 대해 뭐가 좋아?
A What do you like about your boyfrien
B He has a warm heart and a nice voice
A 남자 친구 어디가 좋아?
B 마음이 따뜻하고 목소리가 좋아.

❷ **check out sth** ~를 보러 가다, 가
A Have you been to the new k
Yes. That's cool. You

---

③ 생생한 대화문으로
오늘 배울 주요 표현 익히기

④ 오늘 배울 주요 표현을 활용한
Mini Dialogue로
회화 실력 업그레이드하기

DAY 001~005가
끝나면 **Review Quiz**를 풀면서
탄탄하게 복습하기

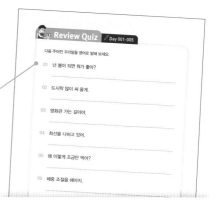

Review Quiz / Day 001-005

다음 주어진 우리말을 영어로 말해 보세요.

01 넌 봄이 되면 뭐가 좋아?
_____

02 도시락 많이 싸 올게.
_____

03 영화관 가는 길이야.
_____

04 최선을 다하고 있어.
_____

05 왜 이렇게 조금만 먹어?
_____

06 체중 조절을 해야지.
_____

기적의 100일 학습 도우미

🎧 **7가지 학습자료
무료 제공**

학습 효과를 극대화하는 7가지 무료 학습자료   www.nexusbook.com

🗣	원어민 MP3	원어민이 직접 녹음한 MP3를 들으며 발음을 체크하고, 상황에 따른 뉘앙스까지 익힐 수 있도록 해 보세요.
🗣	우리말 MP3	우리말 MP3를 들으며 해당하는 영어 표현을 말하는 연습을 해 보세요. 최고의 복습 효과를 볼 수 있습니다.
🎧	리스닝 MP3	중요 문장들을 뽑아 리스닝 테스트를 할 수 있도록 MP3를 구성했습니다. 받아쓰기를 한 후 큰 소리로 따라 말해 보세요.
🎧	리스닝 테스트	[리스닝 MP3]와 함께 활용합니다. 꼭 기억해야 할 문장들만 뽑아 받아쓰기를 할 수 있도록 구성했습니다.
📖	단어 노트	본문에서 헷갈릴 수 있는 단어들을 정리하였습니다. 일부러 사전을 찾지 않아도 바로 단어의 뜻을 확인할 수 있습니다.
👤	단어 Quiz	단어 노트의 학습을 마치고 제대로 익혔는지 확인해 보세요. 헷갈린다면 다시 단어 노트를 펴고 반복해서 익힙니다.
🎙	저자 강의	저자 선생님이 직접 녹음한 강의를 들으며 학습해 보세요. 궁금했던 점을 모두 해결할 수 있습니다.

MP3 & 강의 듣는 방법

1

스마트폰에 QR코드 리더를 설치하여
책 속의 QR코드를 인식하면
원어민 MP3와 녹음 강의를
바로 들을 수 있습니다.

MP3 + 강의

2

유튜브에서 도서명을 검색하면
저자 동영상 강의를 볼 수 있습니다.

3

네이버 오디오클립 어플을 설치하면
MP3를 휴대폰에 다운받을 수 있습니다.

4

팟빵, 아이튠즈 팟캐스트에서
도서명을 검색하세요.

학습 진도표

DAY 001~050

DAY 051~100

DAY
001~005

MP3와 저자 강의를 들어 보세요.

DAY 001

봄꽃 나들이

🎧 Day 001

MP3 강의 듣기

What do you like about spring?

봄이 되면 뭐가 좋아?

A **What do you like about** spring?

B A lot of trees burst into blossom* all across the country*.

A Let's **check out** the cherry blossom festival* tomorrow.

B Sure. We have to leave early to **beat the traffic**.

A I'll call you first thing in the morning*.

B I'll **pack a big lunch** for us.

A 넌 봄이 되면 뭐가 좋아?
B 전국적으로 나무에 꽃이 만개하잖아.
A 내일 벚꽃 축제에 같이 가자.
B 좋아. 일찍 출발해서 교통 혼잡을 피하자.
A 일어나자마자 바로 전화할게.
B 도시락 많이 싸 올게.

기타표현체크

• burst into blossom (꽃이) 만개하다 • all across the country 전국적으로
• cherry blossom festival 벚꽃 축제 • first thing in the morning 일어나자마자, 출근하자마자

16

❶ What do you like about sth/sb?

~에 대해 뭐가 좋아?

A What do you like about your boyfriend?

B He has a warm heart and a nice voice.

A 남자 친구 어디가 좋아?

B 마음이 따뜻하고 목소리가 좋아.

❷ check out sth ~를 보러 가다, 가 보다

A Have you been to the new kids café nearby?

B Yes. That's cool. You should go and check it out.

A 근처에 새로 오픈한 키즈 카페 가 본 적 있어?

B 그럼. 정말 좋던데. 너도 꼭 한번 가 봐.

❸ beat the traffic 교통 혼잡을 피하다

A I should leave now. I want to beat the traffic.

B Oh, it's already past 5. You'd better hurry.

A 난 이제 가 볼게. 차 막히기 전에 가려고.

B 아, 벌써 5시가 지났구나. 어서 서둘러.

❹ pack a (big) lunch 도시락을 (많이) 싸다

A I'm looking forward to our hiking trip this weekend.

B So am I. Don't forget to pack a lunch.

A 이번 주말에 가는 하이킹 기대하고 있어.

B 나도 그래. 도시락 싸 오는 거 잊지 마.

Don't go out of your way.

너무 무리는 하지 마.

A The movie begins at 6. Let's leave around* 5.

B Okay. **The traffic isn't bad** at that time of day*.

A I'll **pick** you **up from** your place.

B Thanks, but don't **go out of your way**.

A No problem*. It's on my way to* the cinema.

B **Give** me **a call** when you're about to leave.

A 영화가 6시에 시작해. 5시쯤 출발하자.
B 좋아. 그 시간에는 차가 안 막히니까.
A 내가 너희 집으로 데리러 갈게.
B 고맙지만 너무 무리는 하지 마.
A 괜찮아. 영화관 가는 길이야.
B 출발할 때 전화해.

기타표현체크

- around+숫자 ~시경에
- No problem 괜찮아, 물론이지
- at that time of day 하루 중 그 시간에는
- on one's way to+장소 ~에 가는 길이다

18

❶ The traffic is (so) bad 차가 (많이) 막히다

A Why is traffic so bad at this time of day?

B There must be an accident somewhere.

A 이 시간에 왜 차가 막히는 거죠?
B 어딘가에서 사고가 났을 겁니다.

❷ pick sb up from + 장소 ~를 ~로 데리러 가다

A What if my flight arrives late at night?

B Your dad will pick you up from the airport.

A 비행기가 밤늦게 도착하면 어떡해요?
B 아빠가 공항으로 데리러 가실 거야.

❸ go out of one's way 일부러 ~하다

A I can give you a ride home. I'm going in that direction.

B Thanks, but you don't have to go out of your way.

A 집까지 태워 줄게. 나도 그 방향으로 가거든.
B 고맙지만, 일부러 그럴 필요는 없어.

❹ give sb a call ~에게 전화하다

A Wait a sec. I'm on the phone at the moment.

B Okay. Please give me a call as soon as you can.

A 잠깐만. 나 지금 통화중이야.
B 알았어. 통화 가능할 때 전화해.

MP3 강의 듣기

DAY 003

No more impulse buying!

충동구매 그만해.

A No more impulse buying*! It's been two hours.

B Don't be so pushy*. I'm **doing my best.**

A Pretty please. Let's just stick to* our shopping list.

B Would you stop it? Don't **try my patience.**

A Let's split up*. I'll **go get some beers.**

B OK. **I'll see you at** the cashier in 10 minutes.

A 충동구매 그만해. 두 시간째야.
B 재촉하지 마. 최선을 다하고 있어.
A 제발 부탁이야. 쇼핑 목록에 충실하자.
B 그만 좀 해. 힘들게 좀 하지 마.
A 일단 흩어지자. 맥주 좀 사 올게.
B 알았어. 10분 후에 계산대에서 만나.

기타표현체크

• impulse buying   충동구매
• stick to sth   ~에 충실하다

• pushy   강압적인
• split up   흩어지다

1 **do one's (very) best** 최선을 다하다

A I don't think I'll be able to be fluent in English.

B You don't need to be perfect. Just try to do your best.

A 난 영어를 유창하게 할 수 없을 것 같아.
B 완벽할 필요는 없어. 그냥 최선을 다해 봐.

---

2 **try one's patience** 인내심을 시험하다

A Can you take your kids outside for a minute?

B Sorry. They were really trying your patience.

A 잠시 아이들 좀 밖으로 데려가 줄래?
B 미안해. 걔들이 널 짜증 나게 했구나.

---

3 **go get some sth** ~을 가지러(사러) 가다

A It's stuffy in here. Let's go get some fresh air.

B Good. I was about to have a coffee break.

A 여기 답답하다. 바람이나 좀 씌러 가자.
B 좋아. 안 그래도 커피 한잔 하려고 했어.

---

4 **I'll see you at[in] sth** ~에서 만납시다

A You need to arrive 3 hours before the departure.

B OK. I'll see you at the airport tomorrow then.

A 출발 3시간 전까지 도착해야 해.
B 알았어. 그럼 내일 공항에서 보자.

Why do you eat like a bird?

왜 이렇게 조금만 먹어?

A What's going on? Why do you **eat like a bird**?

B I'm getting overweight*. I'm trying to **cut down on** carbs.

A I doubt* you can do it. You're a big fan of* carbs.

B Not any more. I have to **watch my weight**.

A I think you look good the way you are*.

B Don't stop me*. I **have my heart set on** doing it.

A 무슨 일이야? 왜 이렇게 조금만 먹어?

B 살이 찌고 있어. 탄수화물을 줄이려고 노력 중이야.

A 할 수 있을까? 너 탄수화물 엄청 좋아하잖아.

B 이젠 아니야. 체중 조절을 해야 해.

A 지금도 괜찮아 보이는 것 같은데.

B 말리지 마. 다이어트하기로 마음먹었어.

기타표현체크

- get overweight   체중이 늘다
- be a big fan of sth   ~를 매우 좋아하다
- Don't stop me   말리지 마
- I doubt 주어+동사   ~ 못할 것 같은데
- the way you are   있는 그대로

22

① eat like a bird 소식하다, 아주 조금 먹다

A You look slimmer than when I saw you last.

B If you want to lose weight, you should eat like a bird.

A 지난번 만났을 때보다 더 날씬해졌네.

B 너도 살 빼고 싶으면 소식하는 게 좋아.

② cut down on + (동)명사 ~를 줄이다

A I have trouble sleeping at night these days.

B You should get up early and cut down on coffee.

A 요즘 밤에 잠을 잘 수가 없어.

B 아침에 일찍 일어나고 커피 좀 줄여.

③ watch one's weight 체중을 조절하다

A This is the best pizza ever. Why aren't you eating?

B Bikini season is coming up. I should watch my weight.

A 지금껏 먹어 본 피자 중 가장 맛있다. 왜 안 먹어?

B 비키니 시즌이 오고 있어. 체중 조절을 해야 해.

④ have one's heart set on + (동)명사
~하기로 마음을 정하다

A Have you decided how to do to learn English?

B I have my heart set on going abroad next month.

A 영어 배우러 어떻게 할지 결정했어?

B 다음 달에 해외에 나가기로 결정했어.

23

I'm feeling a bit bloated.

속이 좀 더부룩해.

A Are you ready to* **go out for** dinner?

B Yes, but I'm **feeling** a bit **bloated.**

A Really? What have you had for lunch?

B I think* I ate some tteokbokki in the afternoon.

A Can I get you something* to **ease your stomach?**

B No, thanks. I'll **have** some porridge* **delivered.**

A 저녁 먹으러 나갈 준비됐어?

B 응. 근데 속이 좀 더부룩해.

A 정말? 점심 때 뭐 먹었는데?

B 오후에 떡볶이를 좀 먹은 것 같아.

A 속 편하게 해 줄 것 좀 사다 줄까?

B 아니, 괜찮아. 죽 배달시킬 거야.

기타표현체크

- be ready to + 동사원형   ~할 준비가 되다
- get sb something   ~에게 ~을 사다주다
- I think 주어 + 동사   ~인 것 같다
- porridge (with crab meat)   (게살)죽

① go out for sth ~하러(먹으러) 가다

A How about going out for a walk with our dogs?

B Great. I'll get some drinks on the way to the park.

A 우리 강아지 데리고 산책하러 갈까?

B 좋아. 공원 가는 길에 음료수 사 줄게.

② feel bloated (속이) 더부룩하다

A I feel bloated. My stomach is full of gas.

B What did I tell you? Stop having late night snacks.

A 속이 더부룩해. 배에 가스가 꽉 찼어.

B 내가 뭐랬어? 야식 좀 먹지 마.

③ ease one's stomach 속을 편하게 하다

A I think I have an upset stomach from dinner.

B Try these pills. They will ease your stomach.

A 저녁 먹은 게 체한 것 같아.

B 이 알약 좀 먹어 봐. 속이 편해질 거야.

④ have sth delivered ~를 배달시키다

A I'm really craving for some fried chicken.

B I read your mind. I just had it delivered.

A 프라이드치킨이 너무 먹고 싶어.

B 네 마음을 읽었지. 방금 배달 시켰어.

25

다음 주어진 우리말을 영어로 말해 보세요.

01 넌 봄이 되면 뭐가 좋아?

----

02 도시락 많이 싸 올게.

----

03 영화관 가는 길이야.

----

04 최선을 다하고 있어.

----

05 왜 이렇게 조금만 먹어?

----

06 체중 조절을 해야지.

----

07 속이 좀 더부룩해.

----

08 점심 때 뭐 먹었는데?

●정답 01. What do you like about spring?　02. I'll pack a big lunch for us.　03. It's on my way to the cinema.　04. I'm doing my best.　05. Why do you eat like a bird?　06. I have to watch my weight.　07. I'm feeling a bit bloated.　08. What have you had at lunch?

DAY
006~010

MP3와 저자 강의를 들어 보세요.

DAY 006

외모가 경쟁력

Day 006

MP3 강의 듣기

You look younger than your age.

넌 나이보다 어려 보여.

A Look at you! It looks like* you got a perm*.

B Yes. Can you tell*? How do I look?

A It looks great. You **look younger than your age.**

B Really? That's what **I've always wanted.**

A You're really into* **taking care of your looks.**

B I have a date* tonight. I want to **leave a good impression.**

A 웬일이야. 파마한 것 같은데.

B 맞아. 알아보겠어? 어때 보여?

A 보기 좋은데. 나이보다 어려 보여.

B 정말? 그게 내가 늘 바라던 거야.

A 외모 관리에 너무 신경 쓰는데.

B 저녁에 데이트가 있어. 좋은 인상을 남겨야지.

기타표현체크

- It looks like 주어+동사　～한 것 같다
- tell　구별하다, 알아차리다
- have a date (with sb)　～와 데이트를 하다
- get a perm　파마를 하다
- be into+(동)명사　～에 관심이 많다, 좋아하다

28

1 look younger than one's age 나이보다 어려 보이다

A Why do women spend hours putting on their make-up.

B Because they want to look younger than their age.

A 여자들은 왜 화장하는 데 몇 시간씩 걸리는 거야?

B 자신의 나이보다 더 젊어 보이고 싶으니까 그렇지.

2 I've always wanted to+동사원형 난 늘 ~하고 싶었어

A I'm thinking of taking guitar lessons. Want to join me?

B Great! I've always wanted to learn how to play the guitar.

A 기타 강습 받으려고 하는데. 같이 할래?

B 좋지! 난 늘 기타 치는 법을 배우고 싶었어.

3 take care of one's looks[appearance]
외모를 관리하다

A I think Koreans are good at taking care of their looks.

B They dress well and can't stand looking tacky.

A 한국인들은 외모 관리를 잘하는 것 같아.

B 옷을 잘 입고 촌스러워 보이는 걸 못 참지.

4 leave[make] a good impression
좋은 인상을 남기다

A Can you tell me how to make a good impression?

B I just try to smile a lot and look confident.

A 좋은 인상을 주는 방법 좀 알려 줄래?

B 많이 웃고 자신감 있게 보이려고 노력해.

DAY 007

It runs every 20 minutes.

20분마다 운행합니다.

A **How can I get to** the Express Bus Terminal*?

B **You can take the bus No. 3** across the street*.

A **You mean I have to** cross the road?

B Right. From what I know*, **it runs every 20 minutes**.

A Thank you. There comes* the bus.

B The traffic light is green. Run!

A 고속버스 터미널까지 어떻게 가나요?
B 건너편에서 3번 버스를 타시면 됩니다.
A 도로를 건너야 한다는 뜻이죠?
B 네. 제가 알기로는 20분마다 운행해요.
A 고마워요. 저기 버스가 오네요.
B 신호등이 파란불이네요. 뛰세요!

기타표현체크

- Express Bus Terminal   고속버스 터미널
- From what I know   내가 알기로는
- across the street   길 건너편에서
- There[Here] comes sth   ~가 온다

1 How can I get to +장소 명사? ~까지 어떻게 가나요?

A Excuse me. How can I get to the Namsan Tower?

B You can take the shuttle bus at the Seoul station.

A 실례합니다. 남산타워는 어떻게 가나요?

B 서울역에서 셔틀버스를 타시면 됩니다.

2 take the bus[line] number ~번 버스[지하철]를 타다

A Can you tell me the way to Deoksugung Palace?

B You should take the line No. 2 and get off at City Hall.

A 덕수궁에 가는 길 좀 알려 주시겠어요?

B 지하철 2호선을 타고 시청역에서 내리세요.

3 You mean I have to +동사원형? ~해야 한다는 뜻이죠?

A My boss likes it when I ask him to eat out for a change.

B You mean I have to look for some well-known restaurants?

A 부장님은 기분 전환 삼아 외식하자고 하면 좋아하셔.

B 그 말은 내가 유명한 식당을 찾아봐야 한다는 뜻이지?

4 동사+every ~ minutes[hours]
~ 간격으로 ~를 하다

A How do you stay fit? Are you taking supplements?

B No. I eat meals every 5 hours and exercise regularly.

A 어떻게 건강을 유지해? 건강 보조제 복용하니?

B 아니. 5시간마다 식사하고 규칙적으로 운동해.

It's too good to be true.

너무 좋다.

A What a* nice view! It's **too good to be true**.

B Let's take a picture. Did you bring your selfie-stick*?

A Oh, no! I think I left it in* my hotel room.

B Let's **ask someone else to** take one.

A Excuse me. Would you* **take a picture for** us?

B Try to **get the fountain in the background**.

A 전망 진짜 좋다. 너무 좋아.

B 사진 찍자. 셀카봉 가져왔어?

A 이런! 호텔 방에 두고 왔나 봐.

B 다른 사람한테 찍어 달라고 하자.

A 실례지만 사진 한 장 찍어 주시겠어요?

B 배경에 분수가 나오게 찍어 주세요.

기타표현체크

• What a 형용사+명사! 완전 ~하구나

• leave sth in 장소 ~에 ~을 두고 오다

• sefie-stick 셀카봉

• Would you + 동사원형? ~해 주실래요?

32

1 sth is too good to be true ~가 너무 좋다

A My wife is too good to be true. I'm still in love with her.

B You're a devoted husband as well as a good father.

A 난 아내가 너무 좋아. 여전히 사랑해.

B 넌 좋은 아빠이면서 애처가로구나.

2 ask sb to + 동사원형 ~에게 ~를 부탁하다

A He's out of the office for a while. Can I take a message?

B No. Please ask him to call me back when he returns.

A 잠시 자리를 비우셨는데요. 메모 남겨 드릴까요?

B 아니요. 돌아오시면 전화 좀 달라고 전해 주세요.

3 take a picture for sb ~의 사진을 찍다

A Excuse me. Could you take a picture for me ?

B Sure. Say cheese. Three, two, one. (Click!)

A 실례합니다. 사진 좀 찍어 주시겠어요?

B 물론이죠. 웃으세요. 셋, 둘, 하나. (찰칵!)

4 get sth in the background 배경에 ~가 나오게 찍다

A Can you get the Falls in the background?

B Sure. Please take a step back. Good. I'll take it.

A 폭포가 배경으로 나오게 찍어 주실래요?

B 그럼요. 한 걸음 뒤로 가 주세요. 좋아요. 찍을게요.

수제 돈가스

🎧 Day 009

MP3 강의 듣기

My stomach is growling.

배에서 꼬르륵 소리가 나.

A I think this place is the best in town*.

B What's the most popular item on the menu*?

A It's **well-known for** handmade pork cutlet*.

B I can't wait to* eat it. **My stomach is growling**.

A It's coming. **How do you like it?**

B Wow! This **is out of this world**.

A 여기가 동네에서 최고인 것 같아.
B 메뉴 중에 가장 인기 있는 건 뭐야?
A 수제 돈가스가 꽤 유명해.
B 빨리 먹고 싶다. 배에서 꼬르륵거려.
A 음식 나온다. 맛이 어때?
B 와! 진짜 맛있는데.

기타표현체크

· the best in town 동네에서 최고인
· pork cutlet 돈가스

· the most popular item on the menu 최고 인기 메뉴
· can't wait to + 동사원형 빨리 ~하고 싶다

❶ be well-known for + (동)명사 ~로 꽤 유명하다

A Have you heard of the Empire State Building?
B Yes. It's well known for the night view of New York.

A 혹시 '엠파이어 스테이트' 빌딩이라고 알아?
B 그럼. 뉴욕 야경으로 정말 유명한 곳이야.

❷ One's stomach is growling 배가 꼬르륵거리다

A How was school today? You skipped breakfast.
B My stomach was growling in class all morning.

A 오늘 학교에서 어땠어? 아침도 안 먹고 갔잖아.
B 오전 내내 수업 시간에 배가 꼬르륵거렸어요.

❸ How do you like sth?
~는 어때? / (음식) ~는 어떻게 해 드릴까요?

A Dinner is almost ready. How do you like your eggs?
B Sunny side up. Please go easy on the salt.

A 저녁 준비 거의 다 됐어. 달걀은 어떻게 해 줄까?
B 한쪽만 익혀 주세요. 소금은 조금만 넣어 주세요.

❹ be out of this world 훌륭하다, 탁월하다

A The rear camera of the new iphone is out of this world.
B I'm using the previous model. I can't tell the difference.

A 새로 출시한 아이폰 후방 카메라가 정말 끝내줘.
B 난 이전 모델 사용하고 있는데. 별 차이 없던데.

DAY 010

김칫국 마시지 마

🎧 Day 010

I have good vibes this time.

이번에는 느낌이 좋아.

MP3 강의 듣기

A You look sharp* today. What's the occasion*?

B My friend **set** me **up on a blind date** tonight.

A Good for you! I hope it works out.

B For some reason*, I **have good vibes** this time.

A **Don't count your chickens before they hatch**.

B It's for real*! You can **take my word for it**.

A 오늘 멋지다. 오늘 무슨 날이야?

B 오늘 저녁에 친구가 소개팅을 주선해 줬어.

A 잘됐네! 잘되면 좋겠다.

B 이번엔 왠지 느낌이 좋아.

A 김칫국 좀 마시지 마.

B 진짜야. 내 말 믿어도 돼.

기타표현체크

· **look sharp** 멋져 보이다
· **for some reason** 왠지 모르지만

· **occasion** (특별한) 날, 행사
· **It's for real** 정말이야, 진짜야

36

1. set sb up on a blind date ~에게 소개팅을 주선하다

A This year is almost over. I don't want to let it pass by.

B I'm gonna set you up on a blind date with my colleague.

A 올해가 다 갔어. 이렇게 보내고 싶지 않은데.
B 내가 회사 동료 중 한 명을 소개해 줄게.

2. have good vibes (about sth) ~에 대해 좋은 느낌이 들다

A It's spacious. I have good vibes about this house.

B That's good to hear. Let's make a contract this week.

A 꽤 넓군요. 이 집은 느낌이 좋아요.
B 다행이네요. 이번 주에 계약하시죠.

3. Don't count your chickens before they hatch. 김칫국부터 마시지 마라

A I think I can make some money in stocks this month.

B I doubt it. Don't count your chickens before they hatch.

A 이번 달에 주식으로 돈 좀 벌 수 있을 것 같아.
B 과연 그럴까? 김칫국부터 마시지 마.

4. (You can) take my word for it 내 말 믿어도 돼

A How do I know you're telling the truth?

B Take my word for it. You won't regret it.

A 네 말이 진짜인지 내가 어떻게 알아?
B 내 말 좀 믿어봐. 후회하지 않을 거야.

다음 주어진 우리말을 영어로 말해 보세요.

01 어때 보여?

----

02 좋은 인상을 남겨야지.

----

03 고속버스 터미널까지 어떻게 가나요?

----

04 저기 버스가 오네요.

----

05 사진 한 장 찍어 주시겠어요?

----

06 배에서 꼬르륵 소리가 나.

----

07 맛이 어때?

----

08 내 말 믿어도 돼.

● 정답 01. How do I look?   02. I want to leave a good impression   03. How can I get to the Express Bus Terminal?   04. There comes the bus.   05. Would you take a picture for us?   06. My stomach is growling. 07. How do you like it?   08. You can take my word for it.

DAY
011~015

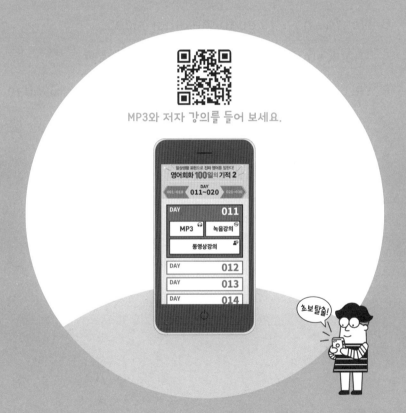

MP3와 저자 강의를 들어 보세요.

Do I need to change trains?

MP3 강의 듣기

열차를 갈아타야 하나요?

A **Is this the right way to** Suseo station?

B No. You have to go to the other side*.

A Thank you. Do I need to change trains*?

B Yes. You can **transfer to line number 3** at Gyodae.

A **That's so nice of you.** Thanks a million*.

B Not at all*. **It's my pleasure to** help you.

A 이쪽이 수서역 가는 길이 맞나요?
B 아니요. 반대편으로 가셔야 합니다.
A 고맙습니다. 열차를 갈아타야 하나요?
B 네. 교대역에서 3호선으로 갈아타세요.
A 정말 친절하시네요. 너무 감사합니다.
B 천만에요. 도움이 돼서 기뻐요.

기타표현체크

· go to the other side   반대편으로 가다
· Thanks a million   정말 감사합니다
· change trains   열차를 갈아타다
· Not at all   천만에요

❶ Is this the right way to + 장소? 이쪽이 ~ 방향인가요?

A Is this the right way to **the train station?**

B **Yes. It will take about 20 minutes on foot.**

A 이 방향이 기차역으로 가는 길이 맞나요?
B 네, 맞아요. 걸어서 20분 정도 걸릴 거예요.

❷ transfer to line[bus] number + 숫자
~번 열차[버스]로 갈아타다

A **Hello. How can I get to Korea town from here?**

B **Get off at the next stop and** transfer to bus number 3.

A 안녕하세요. 여기서 한인타운까지 어떻게 가죠?
B 다음 정거장에서 내려서 3번 버스로 갈아타세요.

❸ That's so + 형용사 + of sb 정말 ~하시네요

A That's so **sweet** of **you to give me a gift.**

B **It's nothing. Let me know if you need anything.**

A 나에게 선물을 주다니 참 자상하구나.
B 별거 아니야. 필요한 거 있으면 말해.

❹ (It's my) pleasure to + 동사원형 ~하게 되어 기뻐요

A **I'm Mr. Hong. I work in the sales department.**

B Pleasure to **meet you. I've heard a lot about you.**

A 미스터 홍입니다. 영업부서에서 일합니다.
B 뵙게 되어 기뻐요. 말씀 많이 들었습니다.

I wouldn't miss it for the world.

무슨 일이 있어도 참석해야지.

A I'm **throwing a birthday party** for Joy on Friday. Can you come?

B Are you kidding? I **wouldn't miss it for the world**.

A I'll invite some of my friends from university*.

B I can **make contact with** some guys if you're okay*.

A Thanks, but we'll be having a small party*.

B That **sounds even better**. It sounds like fun*.

A 금요일에 조이의 생일 파티를 할 거야. 올 수 있어?
B 농담해? 무슨 일이 있어도 참석해야지.
A 대학교 동창들 몇 명 초대할 거야.
B 네가 괜찮다면 몇 명 연락해 볼게.
A 고맙지만 조촐하게 하려고.
B 그럼 더 좋지. 재미있겠다.

기타표현체크

- friends from university   대학교 동창들
- have a small party   파티를 조촐하게 하다
- if you're okay (with it)   네가 괜찮다면
- (It) sounds like fun   재미있을 것 같다

42

Mini Dialogues

❶ throw[have] a (birthday) party

(생일) 파티를 열다

A We're finally done with the exam. Let's have a party.

B I'm not in the mood. I messed up on my test.

A 드디어 시험 끝났다. 우리 파티 하자.

B 그럴 기분이 아니야. 시험을 완전 망쳤어.

❷ wouldn't miss it for the world 반드시 ~할거야

A Are you coming on the camping trip this time?

B Sure. I wouldn't miss it for the world.

A 이번에 캠핑 같이 갈래?

B 물론이지. 무슨 일이 있어도 갈게.

❸ make contact with sb ~와 연락하다

A What is it? It's really hard to make contact with you.

B I rarely answer the phone. Text me if possible.

A 뭐야? 너랑 연락하기 정말 힘들다.

B 나는 전화를 잘 안 받아. 되도록 문자로 해.

❹ sound even[much] better 훨씬 더 좋은 것 같다

A He is a great singer. His rapping sounds even better.

B That's true. I'm so jealous of people who can sing well.

A 그는 노래를 정말 잘해. 랩 부분은 훨씬 더 좋은 것 같아.

B 맞아. 난 노래 잘하는 사람들이 정말 부럽더라.

오늘 휴가 냈어

MP3 강의 듣기

I have the day off.

오늘 쉬는 날이야.

A Honey, wake up! Don't you have work today?

B Didn't I tell you?* I **have the day off**.

A No. You didn't tell me that.

B I've been forgetful* lately. Shall we **go on a picnic**?

A Great! **How long has it been since** we had a date*?

B Sorry. I've been busy* **writing some reports** .

A 여보, 일어나! 오늘 일 안 해?
B 내가 말 안 했나? 쉬는 날이야.
A 아니. 그런 말 한 적 없는데.
B 요즘 자주 깜빡하네. 나들이 좀 갈까?
A 좋지. 우리 데이트한 지 얼마 만이야?
B 미안. 보고서 쓰느라 좀 바빴어.

기타표현체크

• Didn't I tell you? 내가 말 안 했나?
• have a date (with sb) ～와 데이트하다

• forgetful 건망증이 있는
• be busy -ing ～하느라 바쁘다

44

① have[take] the day off 휴가를 내다, 일을 쉬다

A Tomorrow is my 10th wedding anniversary.

B Did you take the day off for your wife?

A 내일은 결혼 10주년 되는 날이야.

B 아내를 위해 하루 휴가 냈어?

② go on a picnic 소풍(나들이) 가다

A Why don't we go on a picnic this weekend?

B It's scorching hot. Let's go to the water park.

A 이번 주말에 함께 나들이 가는 거 어때?

B 더워 죽겠어요. 우리 워터 파크에 가요.

③ How long has it been since 주어 + (과거)동사?
얼마 만에 ~하는 거야?

A How long has it been since you last came here?

B Well, I think it's been about 10 years.

A 마지막으로 여기 와 본 지 얼마나 됐지?

B 글쎄, 10년쯤 된 것 같은데.

④ write a report 보고서를 작성하다

A Time to get out of the office. Are you working late?

B Maybe. I need to write a monthly sales report.

A 퇴근할 시간이야. 늦게까지 일할 거야?

B 아마도. 월별 판매 보고서를 작성해야 해.

DAY 014

온라인 게임

Day 014

Wi-Fi is not available.

와이파이가 안 터져.

MP3 강의 듣기

A What are you playing? It looks fun*.

B You can play even when* Wi-Fi is not available.

A Good! Can you spell that for me?

B MARVEL. Put it in* on the App Store.

A It's awesome*. This is exactly what I wanted.

B In fact, it's the hottest item among kids.

A 무슨 게임을 하는 거야? 재미있어 보인다.
B 와이파이가 안 될 때도 할 수 있어.
A 좋은데! 철자 좀 알려 줄래?
B 앱스토어에서 'MARVEL'이라고 쳐 봐.
A 끝내준다. 내가 바로 원했던 거야.
B 사실, 아이들에게 가장 인기 있는 거야.

기타표현체크

- looks fun   재미있어 보이다
- put sth in   ~을 입력하다

- even when 주어+동사   ~할 때에도
- awesome   멋진, 굉장한

❶ Wi-Fi is (not) available 와이파이가 (안) 터지다

A Is free Wi-Fi available in the lobby?

B Yes, but the signal is not that strong.

A 로비에서 무료 와이파이가 되나요?

B 네, 근데 신호가 그다지 세지는 않아요.

❷ Can you spell that for me? 철자 좀 알려 줄래?

A Did you download the program I told you about?

B Sorry, I didn't catch the name. Can you spell that for me?

A 내가 얘기했던 프로그램 다운받았어?

B 미안해, 이름을 못 알아들었어. 철자 좀 알려 줄래?

❸ This is exactly what 주어 + 동사 이게 바로 ~했던 거야

A You'll never guess what I got for you. Ta-da!

B Oh, my god! This is exactly what I needed.

A 널 위해 뭘 사 왔는지 상상도 못할 걸. 짜잔!

B 세상에! 이거 정말 내가 필요했던 거야.

❹ be the hottest item among + 복수명사
~에게 가장 인기가 있다

A I got my daughter a new iphone last week.

B It's the hottest item among kids these days.

A 지난주에 딸에게 새 아이폰을 사 줬어.

B 요즘 아이들에게 가장 인기 있는 물건이지.

DAY 015

They don't think much of others.

다른 사람 생각은 별로 안 해.

A Can you come to our team dinner* tonight?

B I'm afraid not*. Something came up.

A My boss told me on short notice*.

B We **have no choice**. I'm sorry I can't **make it.**

A I hate it when* they **set the date** unexpectedly.

B I know. They **don't think much of** others.

A 오늘 밤 부서 회식에 올 수 있어?
B 못 갈 것 같아. 일이 생겼어.
A 부장님이 갑자기 말씀하셨어.
B 어쩔 수 없지. 참석 못 해서 미안해.
A 갑자기 날짜 잡는 거 정말 싫어.
B 맞아. 다른 사람 생각은 별로 안 해.

기타표현체크

- team[staff] dinner 부서 회식
- on short notice 촉박하게, 급하게
- I'm afraid not ~을 못 할 것 같아
- I hate it when 주어+동사 ~하는 게 싫다

48

Mini Dialogues

❶ have no choice 어쩔 수 없다

A You can't go to the meeting if you have a fever.
B I hate to stay at home, but I have no choice.

A 열이 있다면 모임에 못 나오겠네.
B 집에 있고 싶지 않지만, 어쩔 수 없지.

❷ make it (to) sth ~에 이르다, 도착하다

A What's your long-term goal in your life?
B I want to make it to the top in my field.

A 인생에서 장기적인 목표는 무엇인가요?
B 제 분야에서 정상에 이르는 것입니다.

❸ set the date 날짜를 잡다

A Have you set the date for the next meeting?
B No. I'll tell you two weeks in advance.

A 다음 모임 날짜 잡았어?
B 아니. 모임 2주일 전에 말해 줄게.

❹ don't think much of sb/sth ~을 개의치 않다

A I heard your father is ignoring the doctor's advice.
B Yes. He doesn't think much of what everyone says.

A 너희 아버지께서 의사의 충고를 안 들으신다며.
B 그래. 모두의 말을 대수롭지 않게 생각하셔.

다음 주어진 우리말을 영어로 말해 보세요.

01   이쪽이 수서역 가는 길이 맞나요?

----

02   열차를 갈아타야 하나요?

----

03   올 수 있어?

----

04   오늘 쉬는 날이야.

----

05   나들이 좀 갈까?

----

06   철자 좀 알려 줄래?

----

07   참석 못 해서 미안해.

----

08   다른 사람 생각은 별로 안 해.

정답 01. Is this the right way to Suseo station?　02. Do I need to change trains?　03. Can you come?　04. I have the day off.　05. Shall we go on a picnic?　06. Can you spell that for me?　07. I'm sorry I can't make it.　08. They don't think much of others.

DAY
016~020

MP3와 저자 강의를 들어 보세요.

We took the wrong way.

길을 잘못 들었어.

A I think we **took the wrong way.** Check the GPS*.

B Don't worry. **I've got it all under control.**

A You're more directionally-challenged* than I am.

B Okay. I'm gonna pull over* to **get my bearings.**

A Let's ask that woman passing by*.

B Good. It **doesn't hurt to** ask.

A 길을 잘못 든 것 같아. 위치 좀 확인해 봐.
B 걱정 마. 내가 다 알아서 하고 있어.
A 넌 나보다 더 방향 감각이 없잖아.
B 좋아. 차 세우고 위치를 확인해 볼게.
A 저기 지나가는 여자한테 물어보자.
B 좋아. 물어봐서 나쁠 건 없지.

기타표현체크

- GPS(Global Positioning System)   인공위성을 이용하여 자신의 위치를 정확히 알아낼 수 있는 시스템
- directionally-challenged   방향 감각이 없는
- pull over   차를 세우다   · pass by   지나가다

① take the wrong way 길을 잘못 들다

A Where have you been? I've been waiting for an hour.

B I took the wrong way and had to retrace my steps.

A 어디 갔었어? 한 시간째 기다리고 있었어.

B 길을 잘못 들어서 온 길을 되돌아가야 했어.

② I've got it all under control 내가 다 알아서 할게

A It doesn't look like you're going to meet the deadline.

B Please stop worrying. I've got it all under control.

A 넌 마감일을 맞출 수 없을 것 같은데.

B 걱정 좀 그만해. 내가 다 알아서 할게.

③ get[lose] one's bearings 위치를 파악하다[방향을 잃다]

A I get the feeling that we're going around in circles.

B I'm terrible with directions. I just lost my bearings.

A 우리 헤매고 있는 것 같은 느낌이 드는데.

B 내가 길눈이 어둡잖아. 방향 감각을 잃었어.

④ It doesn't hurt to + 동사원형 ~해서 나쁠 건 없다

A Slow down a bit. The slope looks slippery.

B All right. It doesn't hurt to be safe.

A 속도 좀 줄여. 경사로가 미끄러워 보여.

B 알았어. 조심해서 나쁠 건 없지.

Can't you just stop dieting?

다이어트 그만하면 안 돼?

A I feel dizzy*. I think it's low blood sugar*.

B Wait a minute. Would you like some cookies?

A Thanks. Oh, now I'm feeling better*.

B **Can't you just stop** dieting? I**'m concerned about** your health.

A Don't worry. I'll **go grocery shopping**. Do you need anything?

B Get a 6-pack of beer* and **pick up the laundry**.

A 어지러워. 당이 떨어졌나 봐.
B 잠시만. 쿠키 좀 먹을래?
A 고마워. 아, 이제 좀 낫다.
B 다이어트 그만하면 안 돼? 네 건강이 염려돼.
A 걱정 마. 장 보러 갈 건데. 필요한 거 있어?
B 6개짜리 맥주 사 오고 세탁물 찾아와.

기타표현체크

• feel dizzy 어지럽다
• feel better 기분이 나아지다

• low blood sugar 저혈당
• 6-pack of beer 6개짜리 맥주팩

① Can't you just stop -ing? ~좀 그만하면 안 돼?

A Can't you just stop joking **around**?

B Why are you being so grouchy today?

A 농담 좀 그만하면 안 돼?

B 너 오늘 왜 그렇게 투덜대니?

② be concerned about + (동)명사 ~대해 염려하다

A It doesn't feel right even though the exam is over.

B Yes. I'm a little concerned about my math grade.

A 시험이 다 끝났지만 뭔가 허전해.

B 맞아. 난 수학 성적이 좀 염려가 돼.

③ go grocery shopping 장 보러 가다

A We ran out of food. Let's go grocery shopping.

B I'm sorry. I'm supposed to get my hair cut.

A 먹을 것이 떨어졌어. 장 보러 가자.

B 미안해. 미용실에 가기로 되어 있어.

④ pick up the laundry 세탁물을 찾다

A Honey! Where is my navy suit and dress shirt?

B Oh, my! I forgot to pick up the laundry at the cleaner's.

A 여보, 남색 정장하고 와이셔츠 어디 있어?

B 이런! 세탁소에서 세탁물 찾는 걸 깜빡했네.

DAY 018

It's been raining on and off.

종일 비가 오락가락하네.

A It's drizzling*. It's been raining **on and off**.

B I don't like mixed weather*. But the wind has died down.*

A **The weather report says** a typhoon is coming.

B It seems like it**'s only getting worse**.

A I'll **stay in bed all day** watching Netflix tomorrow.

B I can't believe a typhoon is going to ruin* my holiday.

A 가랑비가 내린다. 종일 오락가락하네.
B 변덕스러운 날씨 싫다. 바람은 잠잠해졌어.
A 일기 예보에서 태풍이 온다고 하던데.
B 날씨가 좋아질 것 같지가 않아.
A 내일은 종일 뒹굴면서 넷플릭스나 봐야지.
B 태풍이 휴일을 망치다니 믿기지 않아.

기타표현체크

- drizzle (비가) 보슬보슬 오다
- die down 잦아들다, 줄어들다
- mixed weather 변덕스러운 날씨
- ruin sth ~을 망치다

① 동사 + on and off 불규칙하게 ~하다

A Stop turning the power on and off. You could break it.
B When I turn it off, it's muggy, otherwise it's too cold.

A 전원을 켰다 껐다 하지 마. 고장 날 수도 있어.
B (에어컨을) 끄면 후텁지근하고, 켜면 너무 추워.

② The weather report says 주어+동사
일기 예보에서 ~라고 하다

A The weather report says it will rain tomorrow.
B Maybe we have to cancel our picnic at the zoo.

A 일기 예보에서 내일 비가 올 거라고 하네.
B 동물원 나들이 취소해야 할 수도 있겠다.

③ sth is only getting worse ~가 나아질 기미가 안 보이다

A The economy is not improving. It's only getting worse.
B The government is going to offer stimulus money soon.

A 경기가 좋아지질 않아. 나아질 기미가 안 보이네.
B 정부가 곧 경기 부양 자금을 지원할 거야.

④ stay in bed all day 하루 종일 뒹굴다

A My body aches all over. I'm not faking being sick.
B You should stay in bed all day. I'll call your teacher.

A 온 몸이 쑤시고 아파요. 꾀병이 아니에요.
B 하루 종일 누워 있어. 선생님께 전화 할게.

DAY 019

느낌이 필요해

There is no chemistry between us.

우리는 서로 통하는 게 없어.

MP3 강의 듣기

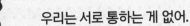

A How did your blind date go*? How is the man?

B He **has a good sense of humor** and cracks me up*.

A Do you want to **get serious with him**?

B Well, but there's something **getting on my nerves.**

A You're so picky. What on earth* is the matter?

B **There was no chemistry between us.**

A 소개팅 어떻게 됐어? 그 남자 어때?
B 유머 감각이 뛰어나고 정말 재미있어.
A 그 사람과 진지하게 만나 볼 거야?
B 글쎄, 근데 신경 쓰이는 게 있어.
A 까다롭기는. 도대체 뭐가 문제야?
B 뭔가 서로 통하는 게 없더라고.

기타표현체크

• How did sth go? ~는 어떻게 됐어?
• What(Who) on earth   도대체 뭐가(누가)

• crack sb up   ~를 웃기다

❶ have a (good) sense of humor 유머 감각이 좋다

A What is your new teacher like? Do you like him?

B Yes. He has a good sense of humor.

A 새로운 선생님 어때? 맘에 들어?

B 응. 정말 유머 감각이 좋으셔.

---

❷ get serious with sb ~와 (진지하게) 사귀다

A How was your date? He wants to see you again.

B I don't want to get serious with him. He's not my type.

A 데이트 어땠어? 그가 널 다시 만나고 싶데.

B 그 사람과 사귀고 싶지 않아. 내 취향이 아니야.

---

❸ get on one's nerves ~의 신경을 건드리다

A It's none of your business. Please leave me alone.

B I'm sorry. I didn't mean to get on your nerves.

A 네가 참견할 일이 아니야. 좀 내버려 둬.

B 미안해. 신경 쓰이게 할 의도는 없었어.

---

❹ There is (no) chemistry between + 복수 명사
서로 (안) 통하다

A What do you think about the movie, *Parasite*?

B I think there was good chemistry between the actors.

A 영화 〈기생충〉에 대해 어떻게 생각해?

B 배우들끼리 호흡이 좋았던 것 같아.

DAY 020

야식 먹고 싶어

Day 020

MP3 강의 듣기

Haven't you had dinner yet?

아직 저녁 안 먹었어?

A **Is there anything to** eat at home?

B It's past 9 p.m. **Haven't you had** dinner yet?

A I shouldn't have had pizza late in the afternoon*.

B Let's see. **Do you want some** instant noodles*?

A I can **make do with** it. But it has passed the expiration date.

B I'll go get* some at the convenience store*.

A 집에 먹을 거 좀 있어?
B 밤 9시가 넘었잖아. 아직 저녁 안 먹었어?
A 오후 늦게 피자를 먹지 말았어야 했는데.
B 어디 보자. 라면이라도 좀 먹을래?
A 그걸로 때워야겠다. 근데 유통 기한이 지났어.
B 내가 편의점 가서 좀 사 올게.

기타표현체크

· late in the afternoon 오후 늦게
· go get sth ~를 사오다

· instant noodles 라면
· convenience store 편의점

60

❶ Is there anything to +동사원형? ~할 거 좀 있나요?

A I'm thirsty. Is there anything to drink?

B How about some milk or orange juice?

A 목말라. 마실 것 좀 있어?
B 우유나 오렌지 주스 줄까?

❷ Have you had +식사명? 식사하셨어요?

A Have you had lunch by any chance?

B Not yet. I was busy working on something.

A 혹시 점심 식사하셨어요?
B 아니요. 뭐 좀 하느라 바빴어요.

❸ Do you want some +음식? ~좀 먹을래?

A Do you want some pizza? I can make it for you.

B Really? When did you learn how to make pizza?

A 피자 좀 먹을래? 내가 만들어 줄게.
B 정말? 피자 요리하는 법은 언제 배웠어?

❹ make do with sth ~로 대충 때우다

A Hurry up! I think the train is coming soon.

B I don't have time to eat. I'll make do with a hotdog.

A 서둘러! 기차가 곧 도착할 것 같아.
B 먹을 시간이 없네. 핫도그로 때워야지.

다음 주어진 우리말을 영어로 말해 보세요.

01 내가 다 알아서 하고 있어.

----

02 물어봐서 나쁠 건 없지.

----

03 어지러워.

----

04 네 건강이 염려돼.

----

05 변덕스러운 날씨 싫다.

----

06 소개팅 어떻게 됐어?

----

07 집에 먹을 거 좀 있어?

----

08 아직 저녁 안 먹었어?

●정답 01. I've got it all under control.　02. It doesn't hurt to ask.　03. I feel dizzy.　04. I'm concerned about your health.　05. I don't like mixed weather.　06. How did your blind date go?　07. Is there anything to eat at home?　08. Haven't you had dinner yet?

DAY
021~025

MP3와 저자 강의를 들어 보세요.

I've searched high and low.

살살이 찾아봤어.

A Oh, no. That's $200 **down the drain.**

B Have you lost* something or what?

A I think I left my sunglasses in* the rest area.

B You **left** them **behind**? Stop **pulling my leg.**

A I'm positive*. I've **searched high and low.**

B You were showing them off* all the time.

A 이런. 200달러를 날리게 생겼네.
B 뭘 잃어버리기라도 했어?
A 휴게소에 선글라스를 두고 온 것 같아.
B 두고 왔다고? 농담하지 마.
A 확실해. 샅샅이 찾아봤어.
B 시도 때도 없이 자랑하더니.

기타표현체크

• lose sth ~을 잃다
• I'm positive 확실해

• leave sth in+장소 ~에 ~을 두고 오다
• show (sth) off ~을 자랑하다

❶ be[go] down the drain 날리다; 헛되이 되다

A I'll give up on my dream of becoming a doctor.
B Oh, dear! All your efforts will go down the drain.

A 난 의사가 되려는 꿈을 포기할 거야.
B 이런! 모든 노력이 수포로 돌아가겠네.

❷ leave sth behind ~를 두고 오다

A Where are the travel brochures I brought?
B I guess I left them behind in the hotel room.

A 내가 가져온 여행 책자 어디 있어?
B 호텔 방에다 두고 온 것 같은데.

❸ pull one's leg 놀리다, 농담하다

A I'll cut back your allowance starting Monday.
B Are you pulling my leg? It's April Fool's Day.

A 월요일부터 네 용돈을 줄일 거야.
B 농담이시죠? 오늘 만우절이잖아요.

❹ search high and low 샅샅이 찾다

A Where is my selfie-stick? I've searched high and low.
B I think I saw it in the corner behind the wardrobe.

A 내 셀카봉 어디 있어? 구석구석 다 찾았어.
B 옷장 뒤 모서리에서 본 것 같은데.

What are friends for?

친구 좋다는 게 뭐야?

A Do you **have any plans for** lunch?

B Not yet. Why don't we **eat out for a change**?

A I know a great place. It looks like a hole in the wall*, but it's tried-and-true*.

B I got it*. You treated me last time.

A We don't have to **take turns. What are friends for?**

B I can buy something cheap. You pay for dinner* instead.

A 점심 약속 있어?
B 아직. 오랜만에 나가서 먹을까?
A 좋은 곳을 알고 있어. 작은 맛집인데, 검증된 곳이야.
B 내가 살게. 지난번에 네가 샀잖아.
A 번갈아 가며 사지 않아도 돼. 친구 좋다는 게 뭐야?
B 싼 거는 내가 살게. 대신 넌 저녁 사.

기타표현체크

- a hole in the wall   좁고 허름한 맛집
- I got it   내가 살게
- tried-and-true   검증된, 믿을 수 있는
- pay for dinner   저녁 식사 값을 내다

① have any plans for sth ~에 대한 약속[계획]이 있다

A Are you busy after work the day after tomorrow?
B I don't have any plans. Why do you ask?

A 내일 모레 퇴근 후에 바쁘니?
B 특별한 건 없어. 왜 그러는데?

② eat out for a change 오랜만에 외식하다

A I've lost my appetite. Let's eat out for a change.
B It's really hot today. How about cold noodles?

A 입맛이 없어. 오랜만에 외식이나 하자.
B 오늘 정말 덥다. 냉면 어때?

③ take turns (-ing) 번갈아 가며 ~하다

A Do you know how long it will take to Busan?
B Approximately 4 hours. Let's take turns driving.

A 부산까지 가는 데 시간이 얼마나 걸리는지 알아?
B 4시간 정도 걸려. 교대로 운전하자.

④ What are friends for? 친구 좋다는 게 뭐야?

A Can you take care of my dog while I'm away?
B I'm happy to help. What are friends for?

A 내가 없는 동안 강아지 좀 돌봐 줄래?
B 기꺼이 도와야지. 친구 좋다는 게 뭐야?

DAY 023

It's easy on the wallet.

부담 없는 가격이야.

해외여행 추천

🎧 Day 023

MP3 강의 듣기

A I heard you've been to* Danang recently.

B It couldn't be better. I highly recommend* it.

A You got the plane ticket from a low-cost carrier*?

B Yeah. It's easy on the wallet. It only cost around $300.

A I'm thrilled to hear it. How about the local cuisine*?

B Mostly the food was not to my taste.

A 최근 다낭에 다녀왔다면서?
B 정말 좋았어. 강력 추천해.
A 비행기표를 저가 항공사에서 구했어?
B 응. 저렴해. 300달러 정도만 들었어.
A 듣기만 해도 설렌다. 현지 음식은 어땠어?
B 대체로 내 입맛에 맞지는 않았어.

기타표현체크

- have been to + 장소 ~에 다녀왔다, 가 봤다
- low-cost carrier 저가 항공사
- I highly recommend sth ~을 적극 추천하다
- local cuisine 현지 음식

68

➊ (sth) couldn't be better 매우 좋다, 더할 나위 없다

A How is everything going in your department?

B Things couldn't be better. How are you doing?

A 네 부서 일은 어떻게 되고 있어?

B 매우 잘 진행되고 있어. 넌 어때?

➋ be easy on the wallet 저렴하다, 부담이 적다

A I'm thinking of getting a new tent for camping.

B How about the one I bought? It's easy on the wallet.

A 캠핑 텐트를 새로 구입하려고 생각 중이야.

B 내가 구입한 건 어때? 가격이 저렴해.

➌ be thrilled to + 동사원형 ~해서 너무 신나(좋아)

A You are choosy. What did you see in her?

B I was thrilled to see her beautiful eyes.

A 너 엄청 까다롭잖아. 그녀의 뭐가 좋았어?

B 그녀의 예쁜 눈을 볼 때 너무 좋았어.

➍ be (not) to one's taste

~의 입맛에 (안) 맞다, 취향이다(아니다)

A What do you think of this kind of music?

B I like pop songs. Classic music is not to my taste.

A 이런 종류의 음악은 어떻게 생각해?

B 팝송이 좋아. 클래식은 내 취향이 아니야.

국물이 시원하다

🎧 Day 024

It hits the spot.

MP3 강의 듣기

내 입맛에 딱이야.

A It **hits the spot.** It's relieving my hangover*.

B You look* terrible. Why did you drink so much?

A **No matter how** much I drink, it never gets old*.

B I'm worried that* you could **get addicted to** alcohol.

A Thanks for your concern. Let's **go grab some coffee**.

B Let's go to the place at the shopping mall.

A 바로 이거야. 숙취가 좀 풀린다.
B 상태가 안 좋네. 왜 그렇게 많이 마셨어?
A 아무리 마셔도 질리지 않는 걸.
B 네가 알코올에 중독될까 걱정돼.
A 걱정해 줘서 고마워. 커피 마시러 가자.
B 쇼핑몰에 있는 곳으로 가자.

기타표현체크

• relieve one's hangover 숙취가 풀리다
• it never gets old 질리지 않다

• look+형용사 ~하게 보이다
• I'm worried that 주어+동사 ~할까 걱정되다

❶ Sth hits the spot 바로 이거야, 딱 좋아

A I love this place. I'm a huge fan of their sushi.

B I'm not easily satisfied, but it really hits the spot.

A 여기 완전 좋아. 난 여기 초밥 정말 좋아해.

B 내가 쉽게 만족 안 하는데, 여기 정말 좋다.

❷ No matter how + 형용사(부사)+주어+동사

아무리 ~하더라도

A No matter how safe it is, it's dangerous at night.

B That's why I've been learning martial arts.

A 아무리 안전하다 해도, 밤에는 위험해.

B 그래서 무술을 배우고 있는 있잖아.

❸ get addicted to sth ~에 중독되다

A I've been getting addicted to American dramas.

B You're into them. Is there a good one these days?

A 나 미국 드라마에 중독되고 있어.

B 푹 빠졌구나. 요즘 볼만한 거 있어?

❹ go grab some coffee 커피 마시러 가다

A How about we go grab some coffee after lunch?

B Good. I know a new place around the corner.

A 점심 식사 후에 커피 한잔 하러 갈래?

B 좋아. 근처에 새로 생긴 곳을 알고 있어.

I may have to take a part-time job.

아르바이트를 해야 할지도 몰라.

A My wife quit her job to be a stay-at-home mom*.

B She has been struggling with* looking after* her kids.

A I may have to take a part-time job for tuition*.

B That's why double-income families* are common nowadays.

A Thanks for listening. It feels good to get that off my chest.

B Shooting the breeze is the only way we can relieve stress.

A 아내가 전업주부가 되려고 퇴사를 했어.
B 그동안 아이들 돌보느라 힘들어했지.
A 교육비 때문에 아르바이트라도 해야 할지 모르겠어.
B 그래서 요즘 맞벌이 가정이 보편화된 거야.
A 들어 줘서 고마워. 털어놓으니 기분 좋다.
B 수다 떠는 게 유일한 스트레스 해소법이지.

기타표현체크

- stay-at-home mom   전업주부
- look after sb/sth   ~를 돌보다
- double-income family   맞벌이 가정
- struggle with + (동)명사   ~로 힘들어하다
- tuition   교육비

① take a part-time job 아르바이트를 하다

A I heard you're taking a year off from school.
B I think I'll take a part-time job for the time being.

A 너 일 년 동안 휴학한다면서.
B 당분간 아르바이트 좀 하려고 해.

② get sth off one's chest 고민을 털어놓다

A What's wrong? You should get it off your chest.
B To be honest, I don't think you can do it.

A 무슨 일인데? 다 터놓고 얘기해 봐.
B 솔직히, 넌 그걸 못할 거라고 생각해.

③ shoot the breeze 수다 떨다, 잡담하다

A What are you doing on your lunch break?
B Not much. Let's shoot the breeze over coffee.

A 점심시간에 뭐 할 거 있어?
B 별일 없어. 커피 마시며 수다 떨자.

④ relieve stress 스트레스를 해소하다

A What do you usually do to relieve stress?
B I work out at the gym and take a cold shower.

A 넌 보통 스트레스를 풀기 위해 무엇을 하니?
B 헬스장에서 운동하고 찬물로 샤워를 해.

Review Quiz ✏ Day 021-025

다음 주어진 우리말을 영어로 말해 보세요.

01 200달러를 날리게 생겼네.

----

02 확실해.

----

03 점심 약속 있어?

----

04 친구 좋다는 게 뭐야?

----

05 강력 추천해.

----

06 숙취가 좀 풀린다.

----

07 커피 마시러 가자.

----

08 수다 떠는 게 유일한 스트레스 해소법이지.

정답 01. That's $200 down the drain. 02. I'm positive. 03. Do you have any plans for lunch? 04. What are friends for? 05. I highly recommend it. 06. It's relieving my hangover. 07. Let's go grab some coffee. 08. Shooting the breeze is the only way we can relieve stress.

DAY
026~030

MP3와 저자 강의를 들어 보세요.

DAY 026

They're out of season.

제철이 아니야.

A Did you see the price of these fruits?

B It's expensive. I think they**'re out of season**.

A We can **get** them **for the best price** near our place.

B **What do we do with** the leftovers* at home?

A We can put them in the blender* to make a juice.

B Let's get some dumplings*. I'll **be in the** frozen food* **aisle**.

A 여기 과일 가격 봤어?
B 비싸다. 제철이 아니라 그래.
A 집 근처에서 저렴하게 살 수 있어.
B 집에 남은 과일은 어떻게 하지?
A 믹서기에 넣어 주스 만들면 돼.
B 만두 좀 사자. 냉동식품 코너에 있을게.

기타표현체크

- leftovers 남은 음식
- dumplings 만두
- blender 믹서기
- frozen food 냉동식품

Mini Dialogues

① sth is out of season 제철이 아니다/비수기이다

A Why do you want to go on vacation in June?
B Hotels are cheap because they're out of season.

A 왜 휴가를 6월에 가려고 하는 거야?
B 비수기라 호텔 요금이 저렴하니까.

---

② get sth for the best price ~을 저렴하게 구입하다

A How can I get a house for the best price?
B I think you should shop around a bit more.

A 어떻게 가장 좋은 가격으로 집을 구할 수 있을까?
B 조금 더 돌아다녀야 할 것 같아.

---

③ What do we do with sth? ~는 어떻게 하죠?

A I'm done. What do we do with these leftover ribs?
B We'll have them later after reheating them in the oven.

A 잘 먹었어요. 남은 갈비는 어떻게 하죠?
B 나중에 오븐에 다시 데워서 먹을 거야.

---

④ be in the ~ aisle ~ 코너에 있다

A Honey. Where are you? I'm at the check out counter.
B I'm in the beer aisle. I'll be there in a minute.

A 자기. 어디야? 난 계산대에 있어.
B 맥주 코너에 있어. 금방 갈게.

MP3 강의 듣기

DAY 027
I had my car fixed.

자동차 수리했어.

A I **had** my car **fixed**, but it**'s been giving me trouble**.

B I know the feeling*. **I've been there before.**

A The mechanic can't **sort things out**.

B Everytime I visit, he keeps saying "Let me double-check."

A I've done a lot of thinking*. I have to act now.

B So what?* Are you gonna sue* the car company?

A 자동차 수리했는데, 계속 말썽이네.
B 그 기분 알아. 나도 그런 적 있어.
A 정비사가 해결을 못하네.
B 갈 때마다 그는 "다시 확인해 볼게요"라고 말하지.
A 많이 생각했어. 이제 행동을 해야겠어.
B 어쩌려고? 자동차 회사를 고소할 거야?

기타표현체크

• I know the feeling   그 기분 알아
• So what?   그래서 어쩔 건데?

• do a lot of thinking   많은 생각을 하다
• sue sb   ~을 고소하다

① have[get] sth fixed ~을 고치다

A The copy machine broke down. What do I do?

B It happens sometimes. You can get it fixed for free.

A 복사기가 고장 났어. 어떻게 해야 하지?

B 가끔 그래. 무료로 수리 받을 수 있어.

② sth has been giving sb trouble
~이 계속 말썽이다

A My laptop has been giving me trouble lately.

B Why not use the tablet instead. It's more handy.

A 요즘 내 노트북이 계속해서 말썽이야.

B 대신 태블릿을 사용해 봐. 더 편리해.

③ I've been there before 나도 그런 적 있어

A Since graduation, I haven't found a job for two years.

B I've been there before. I know how tough it is.

A 졸업 후 2년 동안 직업을 구하지 못했어.

B 나도 그런 적 있어. 얼마나 힘든지 알지.

④ sort out sth ~을 해결하다, 정리하다

A I don't think we can sort out this problem right now.

B An emergency debate will be held tomorrow morning.

A 이 문제를 당장 해결할 수는 없을 것 같아.

B 내일 아침에 긴급회의가 열릴 예정이야.

You have a sweet tooth.

단것을 좋아하는구나.

A I **have a craving for** something sweet.

B You **have a sweet tooth.** You want some candy?

A No. I'll have a cheese burger for a snack*.

B That won't **be easy on your stomach.**

A Sometimes I love **getting a taste of** junk food*.

B I see. You can microwave* it over there.

A 뭔가 달달한 게 당기는데.
B 단것을 좋아하는구나. 사탕 먹을래?
A 아니. 간식으로 치즈 버거 먹을래.
B 위장에 부담이 될 텐데.
A 가끔은 인스턴트식품 먹는 게 좋아.
B 그렇구나. 저기 전자레인지에 데워.

기타표현체크

• for a snack   간식으로
• microwave   전자레인지로 데우다

• junk food   인스턴트 음식

 **Mini Dialogues**

❶ have a craving for sth ~가 당기다(먹고 싶다)

A I'm a little hungry. I have a craving for pizza.
B Let's order in. What kind of pizza do you want?

A 살짝 출출한데. 피자가 당긴다.
B 주문하자. 어떤 피자 먹고 싶어?

❷ have a sweet tooth 단것을 좋아하다

A You have a sweet tooth. Take good care of your teeth.
B I always carry around some mouthwash in my bag.

A 단것을 좋아하는구나. 치아 관리 잘해.
B 늘 구강청정제를 가방에 가지고 다녀.

❸ be easy on one's stomach 위에 부담이 없다

A I think I have indigestion so often these days.
B You'd better eat food that is easy on your stomach.

A 요즘 소화가 꽤 자주 안 되는 것 같아.
B 위에 부담 없는 음식을 먹는 게 좋아.

❹ get a taste of[for] sth ~을 맛보다[~의 맛을 알다]

A Dad! Can you play catchball after lunch?
B Now you seem to be getting a taste for baseball.

A 아빠! 점심 먹고 캐치볼하실래요?
B 이제 야구의 맛을 아는 것 같구나.

DAY 029

I'm allergic to animal fur.

동물 털 알레르기가 있어.

A **Look how** cute it is! Can I pet* it?

B Of course. I adopted* it about a month ago.

A Dogs **are high-maintenance** pets.

B Yes, but it's okay because I'm a dog person*.

A **I'm allergic to** animal fur. So I can't keep them*.

B Just **make yourself at home.** I'll get some drinks.

A 어머, 귀여워라! 만져 봐도 돼?

B 물론이지. 한 달 전쯤 입양했어.

A 개는 손이 많이 가는 동물이잖아.

B 맞아, 하지만 난 개를 좋아하니까 괜찮아.

A 난 동물 털 알레르기가 있어. 그래서 못 키워.

B 편하게 있어. 마실 것 좀 가져올게.

기타표현체크

- pet sth/sb ~을 살짝 만져 보다
- dog person 개를 좋아하는 사람
- adopt sth/sb ~을 입양하다
- keep animals 동물을 기르다

① Look how 형용사/부사+주어+동사! 엄청 ~하구나!

A Come over here. There are bluetooth earphones.

B Look how cheap they are! I'll just grab another pair.

A 이리 와 봐. 블루투스 이어폰이야.
B 와! 엄청 싸다. 한 개 더 사야겠다.

② sth is high-maintenance 손이 많이 가다

A What do you think of my new motorcycle?

B I think it's high-maintenance but it looks nice.

A 내 새 오토바이 어떻게 생각해?
B 관리하기 힘들지만 멋진 것 같아.

③ be allergic to sth ~에 알레르기가 있다

A Do you want to have spicy seafood noodles?

B I'd like to, but I'm allergic to seafood.

A 매운 해물 칼국수 먹을래?
B 그러고 싶지만 해물 알레르기가 있어.

④ make yourself at home 편하게 있어

A I'll get you a cup of tea. Make yourself at home.

B Thank you. Can I use your bathroom?

A 차 한잔 갖다 줄게. 편하게 있어.
B 고마워. 화장실 좀 써도 될까?

It went viral.

짝 퍼졌어.

A Somebody put the fake story online*.

B I saw that on Youtube. It went viral.

A Why do they make stuff up* like that?

B They want to draw attention and people fall for* it easily.

A The thing is* some people go over the line.

B That's why we need to have good judgment.

A 누가 가짜 이야기를 인터넷에 올렸어.
B 나도 유튜브에서 봤어. 짝 퍼졌던데.
A 왜 그런 것을 꾸며 낼까?
B 관심 끌고 싶고 사람들이 잘 속으니까.
A 일부 사람들이 도를 넘는 게 문제야.
B 그래서 우리가 똑똑해져야 해.

기타표현체크

- put sth online 인터넷에 올리다
- fall for sth ~에 속다
- make sth up ~을 꾸며 내다
- The thing is 주어+동사 문제는 ~이다

❶ sth goes viral 입소문 나다, 널리 퍼지다

A The new BTS song 'Dynamite' was released last week.
B I know. It went viral globally as soon as it came out.

A BTS의 신곡 '다이너마이트'가 지난주에 발표됐어.
B 나도 알아. 나오자마자 전 세계적으로 쫙 퍼졌어.

❷ draw (one's) attention (to) ~의 관심을 -로 끌다

A I think it's a good way to make a name for yourself.
B I don't want to draw attention to other people.

A 네 이름을 알릴 수 있는 좋은 기회가 될 거야.
B 난 다른 사람들에게 관심을 끌고 싶지 않아.

❸ go[be] over the line 도를 넘어서다

A How could you do that to her? You're insane.
B I have no excuses. I was totally over the line.

A 그녀한테 어떻게 그럴 수가 있어? 제정신이 아니구나.
B 변명의 여지가 없어. 내가 완전 도가 지나쳤지.

❹ have good judgment 판단력이 좋다, 식견이 있다

A There is something attractive about Steve.
B He has good judgment and makes decisions fast.

A 스티브는 끌어당기는 매력이 있어.
B 그는 판단력이 좋고 결정도 빨라.

다음 주어진 우리말을 영어로 말해 보세요.

01 제철이 아니야.

----

02 냉동식품 코너에 있을게.

----

03 자동차 수리했어.

----

04 나도 그런 적 있어.

----

05 뭔가 달달한 게 당기는데.

----

06 동물 털 알레르기가 있어.

----

07 편하게 있어.

----

08 쫙 퍼졌어.

●정답 01. They're out of season. 02. I'll be in the frozen food aisle. 03. I had my car fixed. 04. I've been there before. 05. I have a craving for something sweet. 06. I'm allergic to animal fur. 07. Make yourself at home. 08. It went viral.

DAY
031~035

MP3와 저자 강의를 들어 보세요.

초보탈출!

It's terribly hot.

지독하게 덥다.

A It's terribly hot. This is murder*.

B It's still May, but it's already hot.

A But I **prefer** a hot summer **to** a cold winter.

B That reminds me*, you **don't seem to** sweat a lot*.

A Since you bring it up*, let's **get some exercise**.

B I'll buy an iced coffee after **working up a sweat**.

A 너무 덥다. 살인적이야.
B 아직 5월인데 벌써 덥네.
A 그래도 추운 겨울보다 더운 여름이 좋아.
B 그러고 보니, 넌 땀을 별로 안 흘리는 것 같아.
A 말 나온 김에 운동이나 좀 하자.
B 땀 흘리고 나서 냉커피 한잔 살게.

기타표현체크

• **This is murder**   살인적이야
• **sweat a lot**   땀을 많이 흘리다

• **That reminds me**   그러고 보니
• **Since you bring it up**   말 나온 김에

 **Mini Dialogues**

① prefer A to B B보다 A가 더 좋다

A It seems like you don't drive when you commute.
B I prefer taking the subway to driving my own car.

A 통근할 때 운전을 안 하는 것 같더라.
B 난 운전하는 것보다 지하철 타는 게 더 좋아.

② don't seem to +동사원형 ~하지 않는 것 같다

A Mommy, I have a cough and a runny nose.
B Come here. You don't seem to have a fever.

A 엄마, 기침을 하고 콧물도 나와요.
B 이리 와 봐. 열은 없는 것 같은데.

③ get some exercise 운동을 좀 하다

A What do you usually do on the weekends?
B I catch up on sleep and get some exercise.

A 주말에 보통 뭐하고 보내?
B 밀린 잠을 자거나 운동을 해.

④ work up a sweat 땀을 흘리다

A You work out every day? Don't push yourself too hard.
B It feels good to take a shower after working up a sweat.

A 매일 운동한다고? 너무 무리하지 마.
B 땀 흘린 후 샤워하면 기분이 좋거든.

89

DAY 032

MP3 강의 듣기

Can I ask you a favor?

부탁 하나 해도 될까?

A You know what*? Can I **ask you a favor?**

B Sure. Go ahead*. What is it?

A I'm going to **take a short trip.** Can you watch my dog*?

B No problem. You know I'm a dog person*.

A Thanks for your help. I'll get you a present*.

B **All right if you insist. Have a safe trip!**

A 있잖아. 부탁 하나 해도 될까?
B 그래. 말해 봐. 뭔데?
A 여행을 좀 가려고. 강아지 좀 봐줄래?
B 물론이지. 나 개 좋아하잖아.
A 도와줘서 고마워. 선물 사 올게.
B 정 그렇다면 좋아. 여행 잘 다녀와!

기타표현체크

- **You know what?** 있잖아
- **watch sth** ~을 봐주다
- **get sb a present** ~에게 선물을 사 주다
- **Go ahead** 어서 말해 봐
- **dog person** 개를 좋아하는 사람

90

1 ask sb a favor ~에게 부탁하다

A Can I ask you a favor? I need some help with the report.

B I wish I could help you, but my hands are full right now.

A 부탁 좀 해도 돼? 보고서 쓰는 것 좀 도와줘.

B 도와주고 싶은데, 지금은 너무 바빠.

2 take a (short) trip (단기) 여행을 가다

A Why don't we take a short trip over the long weekend?

B Let's go to Busan. It's been a while since we last went.

A 연휴도 긴데 어디 잠깐 여행 가는 건 어때?

B 부산으로 가요. 가 본 지 꽤 오래됐잖아요.

3 All right if you insist 정 그렇다면 좋아

A You have to come to the party. It's not fun without you.

B All right if you insist. But I can't stay longer than 2 hours.

A 파티에 꼭 와야 해. 네가 없으면 재미없어.

B 정 그렇다면 좋아. 근데 2시간 이상은 못 있어.

4 Have a safe trip! 여행 잘 다녀와!

A I'll take a short trip to Seoul to get medical treatment.

B I'm glad you're recovering. Have a safe trip!

A 병원 치료 받으러 서울에 잠깐 다녀올 거야.

B 회복되고 있어서 다행이야. 잘 다녀와!

DAY 033

과식의 대가

Day 033

MP3 강의 듣기

I haven't hit the gym in ages.

정말 오랜만에 운동하러 왔어.

A I'm so beat*. I haven't **hit the gym** in ages.

B Any special reason for working out that hard?

A I **pigged out** during the holiday. I have to pay for* it.

B You're **looking good for now**. Don't overdo* it.

A I know you're saying that to **make me feel better**.

B No, I'm serious*. I don't know how to lie.

A 너무 힘들다. 정말 오랜만에 운동하러 왔어.

B 운동을 열심히 하는 특별한 이유가 있니?

A 휴일에 너무 많이 먹었어. 대가를 치러야지.

B 지금도 좋아 보이는데. 너무 무리하지 마.

A 나 기분 좋게 하려고 하는 말인 거 알아.

B 아니, 정말이야. 나 거짓말 못하잖아.

기타표현체크

· beat 지친, 피곤한
· overdo 무리하다
· pay for sth 대가를 지불하다
· I'm serious 정말이야

92

① hit the gym (운동하러) 헬스장에 가다

A Look at these love handles! I have to get in shape.
B It's time to hit the gym. I can recommend a good one.

A 이 옆구리 살 좀 봐! 몸매 관리 좀 해야겠어.
B 헬스장 갈 때가 됐네. 괜찮은 데 추천해 줄게.

② pig out (on sth) ~을 과식하다

A Where do you want to go for your birthday party?
B Let's go to the buffet. I want to pig out on sushi.

A 당신 생일 파티하러 어디 가고 싶어?
B 뷔페로 가요. 초밥 실컷 먹고 싶어요.

③ look good (for now) (지금) 좋아 보이다

A Things are not looking good. Where do you invest?
B I'm watching the market. I don't rush into a decision.

A 상황이 안 좋아 보이는데. 넌 어디에 투자해?
B 시장을 지켜보고 있어. 성급히 결정하지 않아.

④ make sb feel better ~를 기분 좋게 하다

A I think my mother is not in a good mood today.
B Help her with the housework. It'll make her feel better.

A 오늘 엄마가 기분이 좀 안 좋은 것 같아.
B 집안일 좀 도와 드려. 기분 좀 나아지실 거야.

DAY 034

You should get back to normal.

원래대로 돌아가야 돼.

A I've put on* 3 kilograms in the past two months.

B Are you kidding? How did that happen?

A I've **picked up a habit of** snacking late at night*.

B It'll harm your health*. You should **get back to normal.**

A You have a point*. I'll try to **kick the bad habit**.

B **Take into account** the ingredients when you eat.

A 지난 두 달간 체중이 3kg 늘었어.
B 농담이지? 어쩌다 그렇게 됐어?
A 밤늦게 군것질하는 습관이 생겼거든.
B 건강을 해치잖아. 원래대로 돌아가야 돼.
A 맞는 말이야. 나쁜 습관을 고칠 거야.
B 먹을 때 식재료도 따져 봐야 해.

기타표현체크

- put on+중량 살이 찌다
- harm one's health 건강을 해치다
- late at night 밤늦은 시간에
- You have a point 일리가 있다

❶ pick up a habit of -ing ~하는 습관이 생기다

A I forgot how to use this program. Show me again.
B I think you should pick up the habit of taking notes.

A 이 프로그램 사용하는 법 잊어버렸어. 다시 알려 줘.
B 넌 메모하는 습관 좀 기르면 좋을 것 같아.

❷ get[go] back to normal 원래대로 돌아가다

A The summer break is over. I'm free from my kids.
B Things are slowly getting back to normal for everyone.

A 여름 방학이 끝났어. 아이들로부터 해방이다.
B 모두 천천히 일상으로 돌아가고 있어.

❸ kick[break] the (bad) habit (나쁜) 습관을 버리다

A I want to quit smoking, but I can't kick the bad habit.
B Once you're addicted to it, it's hard to give it up.

A 담배를 끊고 싶은데 나쁜 습관을 못 끊겠어.
B 일단 흡연에 중독되면, 끊기 힘들어.

❹ take into account + 명사 ~을 고려(감안)하다

A I don't think you're qualified for this job.
B Please take into account my job experiences.

A 당신은 이 자리에 적합하지 않은 것 같은데요.
B 제 직장 경력을 고려하여 주시기 바랍니다.

Can I have a bite?

한 입 먹어도 돼?

A　I'll have my usual*. Jjampong, please.

B　I'll have Jjajangmyeon. **Make it a double, please.**

A　Please make it less spicy* for me.

B　Two servings of* dumplings **to go, please.**

C　Enjoy your meal! [Staff]

A　Smells good*. **My mouth is watering.**

B　Yours looks yummy* as well. **Can I have a bite?**

A　늘 먹던 거 주세요. 짬뽕이요.

B　전 자장면 주세요. 곱빼기로요.

A　제 꺼는 조금 덜 맵게 해 주세요.

B　만두 2인분은 포장해 주세요.

C　맛있게 드세요! (직원)

A　냄새 좋다. 입에 군침이 돈다.

B　네 꺼도 맛있어 보여. 한 입 먹어도 돼?

기타표현체크

- I'll have the usual　늘 먹던 거로 주세요
- two servings[portions] of + 음식　음식 2인분
- looks yummy　맛있어 보이다
- Make it less spicy　좀 덜 맵게 해 주세요
- smells good　냄새가 좋다

1 **Make it a double, please** 곱빼기로 주세요

A Excuse me. Are you ready to order?
B Spicy jjampong. Make it a double, please.

A 실례합니다. 주문하시겠어요?
B 매운 짬뽕 주세요. 곱빼기로요.

---

2 **음식+to go, please** ~을 포장해 주세요

A Hello. What would you like to order?
B Two cheeseburgers and french fries to go, please.

A 안녕하세요. 뭘 주문하시겠어요?
B 치즈 버거 2개와 감자튀김 포장해 주세요.

---

3 **My mouth is watering** 입에 군침이 돈다

A Look at the color. My mouth is watering.
B Watermelon is the best snack in the summer.

A 색깔 좀 봐. 입에 군침이 도는데.
B 여름에 간식으로 수박이 최고지.

---

4 **Can I have a bite[sip]?** 한 입[모금]만 먹어도 돼?

A What does it taste like? Can I have a sip?
B Of course. It's not as good as the previous one.

A 무슨 맛이야? 한 모금 마셔도 돼?
B 물론이지. 예전 것보단 맛이 없어.

다음 주어진 우리말을 영어로 말해 보세요.

01 추운 겨울보다 더운 여름이 좋아.

- -

02 넌 땀을 별로 안 흘리는 것 같은데.

- -

03 강아지 좀 봐줄래?

- -

04 여행 잘 다녀와!

- -

05 너무 무리하지 마.

- -

06 체중이 3kg 늘었어.

- -

07 맞는 말이야.

- -

08 입에 군침이 돈다.

- -

●정답 01. I prefer a hot summer to a cold winter.   02. You don't seem to sweat a lot.   03. Can you watch my dog?   04. Have a safe trip!   05. Don't overdo it.   06. I've put on 3 kilograms.   07. You have a point.   08. My mouth is watering.

DAY
036~040

MP3와 저자 강의를 들어 보세요.

초보탈출!

I'll be back in a flash.

금방 다녀올게.

A Wow! That was a killer*. My heart is still pounding.

B **This is what I call** the waterslide. Let's **try** it **one more time.**

A You've said the same thing three times already.

B Alright. You stay here, and I'll be back in a flash*.

A I **feel sick to my stomach.** I'm feeble with age*.

B So I told you to work out*. **Serves you right**!

A 와! 끝내준다. 심장이 아직도 쿵쾅거려.
B 이게 워터슬라이드지. 한 번 더 타자.
A 너 벌써 똑같은 말을 세 번째 했어.
B 알았어. 넌 여기 있어. 금방 다녀올게.
A 속이 안 좋아. 나이 들어서 체력이 안 좋아.
B 그러게 운동 좀 하라고 했잖아. 쌤통이다.

기타표현체크

- sth is a killer   ~가 끝내준다
- be feeble with age   나이가 들어 연약하다
- in a flash   금방, 눈 깜짝할 사이에
- work out   운동하다

❶ This is what I call sth 이게 바로 ~이지

A Did you see? Ryu hit a grand slam in the 9th inning.

B This is what I call baseball. Nobody knows!

A 봤어? 류가 9회에 만루 홈런을 터뜨렸어.

B 이게 바로 야구지. 아무도 모른다니까.

❷ try one more[last] time (마지막으로) 한 번 더 하다

A Don't give up easily. It's just a temporary setback.

B Thanks for your support. I'll try one last time.

A 쉽게 포기하지 마. 일시적인 실패일 뿐이야.

B 응원 고마워. 마지막으로 한 번 더 해 볼게.

❸ feel sick to one's stomach 속이 안 좋다, 울렁거리다

A I drank so much that I feel sick to my stomach.

B I lost track of how many bars we went to yesterday.

A 너무 많이 마셔서 속이 울렁거려.

B 어젯밤 몇 차까지 갔는지 기억이 안 나.

❹ (It) serves you right! 쌤통이다

A My head is killing me. I still have a hangover.

B It serves you right. I told you to drink in moderation.

A 머리가 너무 아파. 아직도 술이 안 깨.

B 쌤통이다. 적당히 마시라고 했잖아.

Did it get good reviews?

좋은 평을 받았어?

A Do you want to* **go to the movies** this weekend?

B Sure. There's a movie **I've been wanting to** see.

A I **don't have a clue** what's popular lately.

B I **have** one **in mind.** It's just been released*.

A Did it get good reviews* from critics?

B Absolutely! I'll book the tickets online*.

A 이번 주말에 영화 보러 갈래?
B 좋아. 보고 싶었던 영화가 있어.
A 요즘 어떤 영화가 인기 있는지 모르겠어.
B 마음에 둔 게 있어. 막 개봉했거든.
A 평론가들에게 좋은 평을 받았어?
B 물론이지! 온라인으로 예매할게.

기타표현체크

· Do you want to + 동사원형? ～할래?
· get good reviews 좋은 평을 받다

· be released 개봉하다
· book sth online 온라인으로 예약하다

❶ go to the movies 영화 보러 가다

A Do you want to go to the movies after school?

B I'm afraid I can't make it. How about tomorrow?

A 학교 끝나고 영화 보러 갈래?

B 안 되겠는데. 내일은 어때?

---

❷ I've been wanting to + 동사원형 예전부터 ~하고 싶었다

A I'm going to visit Universal Studio next month.

B Lucky you! I've been wanting to go there for a while.

A 다음 달에 유니버설 스튜디오에 갈 거야.

B 좋겠다! 나도 예전부터 거기 가 보고 싶었어.

---

❸ don't have a clue 전혀 모르다

A Do you know how to add subtitles to videos?

B I don't have a clue. I'm terrible with technology.

A 동영상에 자막 넣는 방법 아니?

B 전혀 몰라. 난 기술 쪽은 약하잖아.

---

❹ have sth in mind ~을 마음에 두다

A Where would you like to go for your honeymoon?

B I don't have a particular place in mind.

A 신혼여행 어디로 가고 싶어?

B 특별히 생각해 둔 곳은 없어.

It runs in my family.

집안 내력인가 봐.

A You're really good at swimming.

B My mom made me learn when I was young.

A You're really athletic*. Not everyone is as good as you*.

B I guess it tends to run in my family.

A I've been taking lessons* for two years. But I'm still nowhere near you.

B Don't take it too hard and just enjoy getting better*.

A 너 수영 정말 잘한다.
B 어렸을 때 엄마가 배우게 해 주셨어.
A 운동 신경이 있어. 다 너만큼 잘하진 않아.
B 집안 내력이 있는 것 같기도 해.
A 2년간 강습을 받고 있는데 네 근처도 못 갔어.
B 너무 상심하지 말고 그냥 발전을 즐겨 봐.

기타표현체크

- athletic 운동을 잘하는
- take a lesson 강습을 받다
- be not as good as sb ~만큼 못 하다
- get better 나아지다

① be good at + (동)명사 ~를 잘하다

A You're good at editing videos. How did you learn it?
B To be honest, I got some help from Youtube.

A 너 영상 편집 잘하는구나. 어떻게 배웠어?
B 솔직히 말하면, 유튜브에서 도움 좀 받았어.

② run in one's family 집안 내력이다

A You have a high forehead. You look like your father.
B I guess it runs in the family. My grandfather was bald.

A 너 이마가 넓구나. 네 아버지랑 닮았어.
B 집안 내력인가 봐. 할아버지가 대머리셨어.

③ be still nowhere near sb/sth ~ 근처도 못 가다

A Your English has improved a lot since I saw you last.
B What are you talking about? I'm still nowhere near you.

A 지난번 봤을 때보다 영어 실력이 엄청 늘었네.
B 무슨 소리 하는 거야? 아직 네 근처에도 못 갔어.

④ Don't take it too hard 너무 상심하지 마

A I'm freaking out. I failed the test by one point.
B Don't take it too hard. It will work out in the end.

A 미치겠다. 1점 차이로 시험에서 떨어졌어.
B 너무 상심하지 마. 결국엔 다 잘 될 거야.

DAY 039

나 먼저 가 볼게

Day 039

MP3 강의 듣기

I don't wanna spoil the fun.

분위기 망치고 싶지 않아.

A It's getting too late. I should get going*.

B Stay a little longer. The party **is in full swing.**

A I'd love to, but* I **have an early morning** tomorrow.

B You're going camping* with your family, right?

A Don't tell anyone. I don't want to **spoil the fun**.

B Okay. **I'll see you when you come back.**

A 너무 늦어지네. 슬슬 가 봐야겠어.
B 조금만 더 있어. 파티가 한창이야.
A 그러고 싶지만, 내일 일찍 일어나야 해.
B 가족이랑 캠핑 간다고 했지?
A 아무한테도 말하지 마. 분위기 깨고 싶지 않아.
B 알았어. 다녀와서 보자.

기타표현체크

- I should get going 슬슬 가 봐야겠다
- go camping 캠핑을 가다
- I'd love to, but 주어+동사 그러고 싶지만 ~하다

106

① Sth is in full swing ~가 한창이다

A I can't believe it's still hot. It's already September.
B The heat is in full swing. It's getting hotter by the year.

A 아직도 덥다니 믿기지 않아. 벌써 9월인데.
B 더위가 한창이야. 해가 갈수록 점점 더워지고 있어.

② have an early morning 아침 일찍 일어나다

A We're having a guy's night out. Can you join us?
B I can't stay out late. I have an early morning tomorrow.

A 저녁에 남자들끼리 놀러갈 건데. 같이 갈래?
B 늦게까지는 안 돼. 내일 일찍 일어나야 하거든.

③ spoil the fun 분위기를 깨다

A I'm sorry about the noise. My dogs are out of control.
B You spoiled the fun. You should take the responsibility.

A 시끄럽게 해서 죄송해요. 개들이 말을 안 듣네요.
B 당신 때문에 분위기 망쳤어요. 책임지세요.

④ I'll see you when you come back
다녀와서 보자

A I'm going on a trip for a few days next week.
B Enjoy your trip. I'll see you when you come back.

A 다음 주에 며칠간 여행 갈 거야.
B 잘 갔다 와. 다녀와서 보자.

DAY 040

집안 심부름

Day 040

MP3 강의 듣기

I put my phone on silent.

휴대폰을 무음으로 해 놨어.

A I've been trying to reach you* all morning*, but I **couldn't get a hold of** you.

B I was in a meeting*. I **put my phone on silent**.

A I see. I thought you must've left it at home.

B What's going on? Something important?

A I just **called to ask about** your plans tonight.

B I **have an errand to run**. My wife wants me to* pick up some meat on my way home*.

A 오전 내내 전화했는데, 연락이 안 되더라.
B 회의 중이었어. 휴대폰을 무음으로 해 놨어.
A 그랬구나. 휴대폰을 집에 두고 온 줄 알았지.
B 무슨 일인데? 중요한 일이야?
A 오늘 저녁에 약속이 있나 해서 전화했어.
B 볼일이 있어. 아내가 집에 오면서 고기 좀 사 오래.

기타표현체크

- have been trying to reach sb   ~에게 계속 연락하다
- all morning(day)   오전 내내(하루 종일)   • be in a meeting   회의 중이다
- want sb to + 동사원형   ~가 ~해 주기를 원하다   • on one's way home   집에 가는(오는) 길에

108

❶ can't get a hold of sb ~와 연락이 안 되다

A Have you heard any news about Rachel?
B No. I can't get a hold of her for some reason.

A 레이첼에 대한 소식 좀 들은 거 있어?
B 아니. 무슨 이유인지 연락이 안 돼.

❷ put one's phone on silent (휴대폰) 무음으로 설정하다

A Come on! The meeting is about to start.
B OK. I should put my phone on silent.

A 서둘러! 회의가 막 시작하려고 해.
B 알았어. 휴대폰을 무음으로 설정해야겠다.

❸ call to ask about sth ~에 대해 물어보려고 전화하다

A I'm calling to ask about your schedule tomorrow.
B I'm all booked up this week. How about next week?

A 내일 일정에 대해 물어보려고 전화했어요.
B 이번 주는 일정이 꽉 찼어요. 다음 주는 어때요?

❹ have an errand to run 볼일이 있다, 처리할 일이 있다

A Why can't you come to the baseball game tomorrow?
B I'm afraid I have so many errands to run.

A 왜 내일 야구 경기 관람하러 못 오는 거야?
B 아쉽지만 내일 처리할 일이 좀 많아서.

다음 주어진 우리말을 영어로 말해 보세요.

01 금방 다녀올게.

----

02 나이 들어서 체력이 안 좋아.

----

03 보고 싶었던 영화가 있어.

----

04 내가 온라인으로 예매할게.

----

05 너 수영 정말 잘한다.

----

06 좀 더 있다 가.

----

07 연락이 안 되더라.

----

08 볼일이 있어.

●정답 01. I'll be back in a flash. 02. I'm feeble with age. 03. There's a movie I've been wanting to see. 04. I'll book the tickets online. 05. You're really good at swimming. 06. Stay a little longer. 07. I couldn't get a hold of you. 08. I have an errand to run.

DAY
041~045

MP3와 저자 강의를 들어 보세요.

It can be covered by insurance.

그건 보험으로 처리가 돼.

A Where is my charger? I'm low on battery.

B I think your battery goes out* too quickly.

A To add insult to injury, the screen was cracked.
I guess it's time to change.

B It can be covered by insurance*. You only have to get
your battery changed*.

A I need the latest model for the new features*.

B Alright. A new smartphone is your best friend.

A 내 충전기 어디 있지? 배터리가 얼마 없어.
B 네 배터리는 너무 빨리 소모되는 것 같아.
A 설상가상으로 액정도 깨졌어. 바꿀 때가 됐나 봐.
B 그건 보험 처리가 돼. 배터리만 교체하면 돼.
A 난 새로운 기능 때문에 최신형이 필요해.
B 알았어. 새 스마트폰 정말 좋아하는구나.

기타표현체크

- go out (전등, 배터리) 나가다
- get sth changed ~을 교체하다
- be covered by insurance 보험 처리가 되다
- feature 기능

1 sb be low on sth ~가 얼마 없다

A We're low on gas. Let's drop by the gas station.
B You should've filled the gas tank before we left.

A 기름이 별로 없어. 주유소에 들렀다 가자.
B 출발하기 전에 기름을 채워 놨어야지.

---

2 To add insult to injury, 주어+동사 설상가상으로 ~하다

A How was your first day at work? Did you arrive on time?
B No. I was late. To add insult to injury, I lost my wallet.

A 첫 출근 날 어땠어? 제시간에 도착했어?
B 아니. 지각했어. 설상가상으로 지갑도 잃어버렸어.

---

3 only have to +동사원형 ~하기만 하면 되다

A Can you show me how to use this mic?
B Sure. You only have to push the power button.

A 이 마이크 사용하는 법 좀 알려 줄래?
B 물론이지. 전원 버튼을 누르기만 하면 돼.

---

4 sth is one's best friend ~을 너무 좋아하다

A I think our kids spend too much time on Youtube.
B What can you do? Smarthphones are their best friends.

A 애들이 유튜브에 시간을 너무 많이 쓰는 것 같아.
B 어쩌겠어. 아이들이 스마트폰을 너무 좋아하잖아.

DAY 042

MP3 강의 듣기

I could use a drink.

술 한잔 마시고 싶다.

A It was a tough day*. **I could use** a drink.

B I'm **staying away from** the booze* these days.

A **What's gotten into you?** I'm buying.

B Actually I've **had the runs** for 3 days.

A It must be tough. Did you eat something wrong*?

B Maybe it's the raw meat* I had the other day.

A 힘든 하루였어. 술 한잔 마시고 싶다.
B 요즘 술을 좀 멀리하고 있어.
A 갑자기 왜 그래? 내가 살게.
B 실은 3일째 설사를 하고 있어.
A 힘들겠다. 뭐 잘못 먹었어?
B 며칠 전 먹은 생고기 때문인 것 같아.

기타표현체크

- **tough day** 힘든 하루
- **eat something wrong** (음식을) 잘못 먹다
- **booze** 술, 알코올 음료
- **raw meat** 생고기

❶ I could use sth ~하면 좋겠다

A I'm so tired. I could really use a hot bath.
B Let's get home early. Suddenly it became very cold.

A 정말 피곤하다. 따뜻한 물에 목욕하고 싶어.
B 일찍 들어가자. 갑자기 날씨가 엄청 추워졌어.

❷ stay away from sb/sth ~을 멀리하다, 거리를 두다

A I think our new employee is such a weirdo.
B If you feel uncomfortable, just stay away from him.

A 새로 온 신입사원이 좀 별난 것 같아.
B 부담스러우면, 거리를 좀 두면 되잖아.

❸ What's gotten into you? 도대체 왜 그래?

A You're being nice to me. What's gotten into you?
B Did you notice? I want to borrow some money.

A 갑자기 잘해 주네. 도대체 왜 그래?
B 눈치 챘어? 돈 좀 빌리고 싶은데.

❹ have[get] the runs 설사를 하다

A You don't look very well. Are you okay?
B I don't feel myself. I still have the runs.

A 안색이 별로 안 좋아 보이는데. 괜찮아?
B 몸이 별로 안 좋아. 설사가 멈추지 않아.

DAY 043

Nothing comes to mind.

생각나는 곳이 없네.

A Where are you going on vacation* this summer?

B Nothing **comes to mind**. I'll need to **bring** my dog **along**.

A You probably have to reserve a vacation cabin*.

B I'll grill meat* and dip my feet in a mountain stream*.

A **Your best bet is to** find a way to beat the heat in the summer.

B I want to **spend** some **quality time** with my family.

A 이번 여름휴가는 어디로 갈 거야?
B 생각나는 곳이 없어. 개도 데려갈 건데.
A 펜션을 예약해야 할 것 같은데.
B 고기도 굽고 계곡물에 발도 담글 거야.
A 여름엔 더위 피하는 법을 찾는 게 최선이지.
B 가족들과 뜻깊은 시간을 보내고 싶어.

기타표현체크

• go on vacation   휴가를 가다
• grill meat   고기를 굽다
• reserve a vacation cabin   펜션을 예약하다
• dip one's feet in a mountain stream   계곡물에 발을 담그다

Mini Dialogues

❶ sth comes to mind (생각이) 떠오르다

A It just came to mind. I think I can't get over her.

B Most people have special feelings about their first love.

A 갑자기 생각났는데. 그녀를 잊지 못하는 것 같아.

B 사람들은 대부분 첫사랑에 애틋한 감정을 느끼지.

❷ bring sb/sth along ~를 데리고 가다[오다]

A Thanks for inviting me to your housewarming party.

B No problem. You can bring your friend along.

A 집들이에 날 초대해 줘서 고마워.

B 별말을 다 해. 친구를 데리고 와도 돼.

❸ One's best bet is to + 동사원형 최선책은 ~이다

A A contagious disease is spreading across the country.

B Our best bet is to stay at home and not walk around.

A 전염병이 전국적으로 확산되고 있어.

B 최선책은 집에 머물면서 돌아다니지 않는 거야.

❹ spend quality time 뜻깊은 시간을 보내다

A What are you going to do on parents' day?

B I'll spend quality time with my folks having dinner.

A 어버이날에 뭐 할 계획이야?

B 부모님과 저녁 먹으며 뜻깊은 시간을 보낼 거야.

DAY 044

I got a backup plan.

대안이 있어.

A It's sweltering* in here. **Turn up the AC.**

B They say **the heat will break** by next week.

A Is there a good way to **beat the heat?**

B There is some leftover* watermelon in the fridge.

A It's all empty. We need to get something to eat*.

B I **got a backup plan**. Let's avoid the heat* at the mart.

A 푹푹 찐다. 에어컨 좀 세게 틀어.
B 다음 주면 더위가 한풀 꺾인데.
A 더위를 이길 좋은 방법이 있을까?
B 냉장고에 수박 남은 게 좀 있어.
A 텅 비었는데. 먹을 것 좀 구입해야겠어.
B 대안이 있어. 마트에서 더위를 피하자.

기타표현체크

- sweltering 무더운, 푹푹 찌는
- get something to eat 먹을 것을 구입하다
- leftover (음식 등이) 남은
- avoid the heat 더위를 피하다

① turn up sth ~의 볼륨(온도)을 올리다

A Did you turn on the heater? Can you turn up the heat?
B It's already on. I think there's something wrong with it.

A 보일러 켰어? 온도 좀 올려 줄래?
B 켜져 있어. 뭔가 문제가 있나 봐.

② the heat will break 더위가 꺾일 것이다

A I can't stand the heat. The temperature is over 35°C.
B The weather report says the heat will break by next week.

A 더워 죽을 것 같아. 기온이 섭씨 35도를 넘었어.
B 일기 예보에서 다음 주쯤 더위가 꺾인다고 해.

③ beat the heat 더위를 이겨 내다

A What are your plans to beat the heat this summer?
B I'll go swimming in an outdoor pool with my kids.

A 이번 여름에는 어떻게 더위를 피할 거야?
B 아이들과 야외 풀장에서 물놀이하러 갈 거야.

④ got(have) a backup plan 대안이 있다

A What are you going to do when you quit your job?
B Don't worry too much. I have a backup plan.

A 너 회사 그만두면 뭐할 거야?
B 너무 걱정 마. 대안이 있어.

DAY 045

온라인 쇼핑

Day 045

MP3 강의 듣기

It's packed with people.

사람 엄청 많아.

A I'm going to the wholesale store* to get something.

B It's Saturday. It's going to **be packed with** people.

A I know, but it's much cheaper than anywhere else.

B The point is* you'll end up* **buying** things **in bulk**.

A But we can save time because we don't have to keep*
going back.

B You can **order online.** It'll **save** you **the trouble.**

A 도매점에 뭐 좀 사러 갈 거야.

B 토요일인데. 사람 엄청 많을 거야.

A 알아. 근데 다른 데보다 훨씬 싸잖아.

B 중요한 건 대량으로 사게 된다는 거지.

A 자주 안 가도 되니 시간을 절약하는 거잖아.

B 온라인으로 주문해. 수고를 덜어 줄 거야.

기타표현체크

- wholesale store 도매점
- end up -ing 결국 ~하게 되다
- The point is 주어+동사 내 말은 ~라는 거야
- keep -ing 계속 ~하다

120

① be packed with sth/sb ~로 가득 차다

A I think it was a killer movie. What about you?
B It was really fun. It was packed with humor.

A 대박 영화였던 것 같아. 넌 어땠어?
B 정말 재미있었어. 유머가 넘치던데.

② buy (sth) in bulk ~을 대량으로 구입하다

A They have a lot of promotions at the store these days.
B That can make you buy in bulk and pay a lot more.

A 요즘 상점에서 판촉 행사를 정말 많이 해.
B 그것은 네가 대량으로 구매하게 만들고, 돈을 더 쓰게 만들어.

③ order sth online 온라인으로 주문하다

A I love your jacket. Where did you get it?
B I ordered it online. They offer free delivery.

A 네 재킷 맘에 든다. 어디에서 샀어?
B 온라인으로 구입했어. 무료 배송이야.

④ save sb the trouble (of -ing) ~하는 수고를 덜다

A I'm thinking about signing up for Netflix soon.
B It'll save you the trouble of having to go to the theater.

A 조만간 넷플릭스에 가입할까 생각 중이야.
B 영화관에 가야 하는 수고를 덜어 줄 거야.

다음 주어진 우리말을 영어로 말해 보세요.

01 내 충전기 어디 있지?

----

02 액정이 깨졌어.

----

03 힘든 하루였어.

----

04 생각나는 곳이 없네.

----

05 더위를 이길 좋은 방법이 있을까?

----

06 마트에서 더위를 피하자.

----

07 사람 엄청 많을 거야.

----

08 온라인으로 주문해 봐.

● 정답 01. Where is my charger?   02. The screen was cracked.   03. It was a tough day.   04. Nothing comes to mind.   05. Is there a good way to beat the heat?   06. Let's avoid the heat at the mart.   07. It's going to be packed with people.   08. You can order online.

DAY
046~050

MP3와 저자 강의를 들어 보세요.

MP3 강의 듣기

I really feel like a beer.

맥주 한잔하고 싶다.

A I really **feel like** a beer. What about you*?

B **There's nothing better than** a cold one* after work.

A Let's **shoot some pool** after having some beer.

B OK. **Is there a good place to** go around here?

A I know a place* where we can drink out on the patio*.

B I love those places. Let's go.

A 맥주 한잔하고 싶다. 넌 어때?

B 일 끝나고 시원한 맥주만한 게 없지.

A 맥주 마시고 나서 포켓볼도 치자.

B 좋아. 이 근처에 갈 만한 데 있어?

A 야외에서 마실 수 있는 데를 알고 있어.

B 나 그런 데 좋아해. 어서 가자.

기타표현체크

• What about you? 넌 어때?
• a place where 주어+동사 ~할 수 있는 곳
• cold one 시원한 맥주
• out on the patio 야외 테라스에서

❶ feel like + (동)명사 ~하고[먹고] 싶다

A I feel like some snacks. How about ordering a pizza?

B I had a big lunch. So I don't want to eat anything.

A 간식 좀 먹고 싶다. 피자 한 판 시키는 거 어때?

B 점심을 많이 먹어서 아무것도 먹고 싶지 않아.

❷ There's nothing better than sth
~보다 나은 게 없다

A How was your trip? You must have jet-lag.

B I'm so exhausted. There is nothing better than home.

A 여행 어땠어? 시차 때문에 힘들겠다.

B 정말 피곤하다. 집보다 나은 곳은 없어.

❸ shoot[play] some pool 포켓볼을 치다

A Let's play some pool while we wait for a taxi.

B That's a great idea. I'll meet you downstairs.

A 택시 기다리는 동안 포켓볼이나 치자.

B 좋은 생각이야. 아래층에서 만나자.

❹ Is there a good place to + 동사원형
~할 만한 데 있나요?

A Is there a good place to visit around here?

B I recommend Insadong, the antique shopping street.

A 이 근처에 가 볼 만한 곳이 있나요?

B 인사동 추천해요. 골동품 쇼핑 거리예요.

MP3 강의 듣기

I'm behind in my work.

일이 좀 밀렸어.

A Is everything okay?* Let's talk over coffee*.

B I **have no time for** rest. I have a report to finish.

A I **can't remember the last time** we talked.

B I**'m behind in my work**. It'll only take a few hours.

A Well, you **deserve recognition for** hard work.

B I'm just doing my job*. Stop flattering* me.

A 별일 없지? 커피 마시며 얘기하자.
B 쉴 시간이 없어. 보고서를 끝내야 해.
A 우리가 언제 대화했는지 기억도 안 나.
B 일이 좀 밀렸거든. 몇 시간이면 될 거야.
A 하여튼, 열심히 하는 건 인정받을 만해.
B 그냥 내 일 하는 거야. 너무 칭찬하지 마.

기타표현체크

- Is everything okay? 별일 없지?
- do one's job 자기 일을 하다
- over coffee 커피 마시면서
- flatter sb ~에게 듣기 좋은 말을 하다

❶ have no time for + (대)명사 (부정적) ~할 여유가 없다

A Can you help me with my homework?
B I have no time for that. That's your job.

A 내 숙제 좀 도와줄래?
B 그럴 시간은 없어. 네 일이잖아.

❷ can't remember the last time 주어+동사
언제 ~했는지 기억도 안 난다

A I'm tired of complaining about my low salary.
B I can't remember the last time I got a raise.

A 월급이 적다고 불평하는 것도 이제 지긋지긋해.
B 급여가 오른 게 언제였는지 기억도 안 나.

❸ sb is behind in one's work 일이 밀려 있다

A Do you wanna grab some beer after work?
B I'm sorry but, I'm way behind in my work.

A 퇴근하고 나서 맥주 한잔 하러 갈래?
B 미안한데 일이 너무 많이 밀려 있어.

❹ deserve recognition for sth ~는 인정받을 만하다

A Thank you for giving me this award.
B You deserve recognition for all the work you've done.

A 이런 상을 주셔서 감사합니다.
B 당신이 한 실적은 인정받아야죠.

The heat keeps me up at night.

더위 때문에 밤에 잠을 못 자.

A Hey, **how are you holding up?**

B Just getting by*. The heat **keeps** me **up** at night.

A I think I'm more tired because I **have late nights.**

B I **can't wait until** the summer is over.

A How about going to a valley* this weekend?

B Sounds perfect*! My kids will like it a lot.

A 안녕, 요즘 어떻게 지내고 있어?
B 그럭저럭. 더위 때문에 밤에 잠을 못 자.
A 나는 밤늦게 자니까 더 피곤한 것 같아.
B 빨리 여름이 끝나면 좋겠다.
A 이번 주말에 계곡이나 갈까?
B 좋지. 애들이 엄청 좋아할거야.

기타표현체크

· (Just) getting by 그럭저럭 지내
· Sounds perfect 정말 좋아

· go to a valley 계곡으로 가다

❶ How are you holding up? (힘든 상황) 어떻게 지내?

A You got dumped by her. How are you holding up?

B Well, I don't know. I'm still in shock.

A 그녀에게 차였다면서. 어떻게 지내?

B 잘 모르겠어. 아직도 충격이 남았어.

---

❷ sth keeps sb up ~ 때문에 잠을 못 이루다

A The mosquitoes kept me up all night.

B I got a lot of bites. I feel itchy all over.

A 모기 때문에 밤새 잠을 설쳤어.

B 나도 엄청 물렸어. 온 몸이 가려워.

---

❸ have a late night 밤늦게 자다

A You look sleepy. You yawned twice already.

B I'm tired. I had a late night working on something.

A 졸려 보여. 벌써 하품을 두 번이나 했어.

B 피곤하네. 뭐 좀 하느라 늦게 잤거든.

---

❹ can't wait until+명사[주어+동사]
빨리 ~가 왔으면 좋겠다

A I'm having a slumber party next Monday.

B I'm so excited. I can't wait until then.

A 다음 주 월요일에 파자마 파티를 할 거야.

B 정말 기대된다. 빨리 그때가 왔으면 좋겠다.

DAY 049

I guess they're in a slump.

그들은 슬럼프에 빠진 것 같아.

A Did you watch the baseball game yesterday?

B No, I missed* it. I was in the middle of* something.

A Our team lost it by the score of 6 to 5. It was close*.

B They're on a six-game losing streak. I guess they're in a slump*.

A It's okay. There's always a trade-off.

B Right. They won the Korean Series last year.

A 어제 야구 경기 봤어?
B 아니, 못 봤어. 뭐 좀 하느라고.
A 우리 팀이 6대 5로 졌어. 아슬아슬했어.
B 6연패째야. 슬럼프에 빠진 것 같아.
A 괜찮아. 얻은 게 있으면 잃는 게 있기 마련이지.
B 하긴. 작년에 한국 시리즈 우승했으니까.

기타표현체크

* miss sth ~을 놓치다, 못 보다
* close 아슬아슬한, 아까운
* be in the middle of sth ~을 하는 중이다
* be in a slump 슬럼프에 빠지다

Mini Dialogues

1 **win[lose] sth by the score of** ~의 점수 차로 이기다[지다]

A We lost the finals by the score of 6 to 5.
B I think we just lost because of little mistakes.

A 우리 팀이 결승전에서 6대 5로 졌어.
B 사소한 실수들 때문에 패배한 것 같아.

2 **be on a 게임 수 winning[losing] streak**
~ 연승[연패] 중이다

A I can't believe our team is on a nine-game winning streak.
B They have finally reclaimed the top spot in the ranking.

A 우리 팀이 9연승을 하다니 믿기질 않아.
B 팀 순위도 마침내 1위를 되찾았어.

3 **There is (always) a trade-off**
(언제나) 양면이 있기 마련이다

A Smartphone addiction is a big problem these days.
B There is a trade-off between the benefits and side effects.

A 요즘 스마트폰 중독이 큰 문제야.
B 혜택과 부작용이라는 양면이 있게 마련이지.

4 **win[lose] the ~ Series** ~ 시리즈에서 우승[패배]하다

A Chicago won the World Series for the third time.
B The final game was so close. It was a real cliffhanger.

A 시카고가 월드시리즈에서 역대 세 번째로 승리했어.
B 마지막 경기는 박빙이었어. 손에 땀을 쥐게 했지.

We're almost halfway through the year.

올해도 거의 절반이나 지났어.

A We're almost halfway through the year.

B The older we get, the faster time seems to go.

A Right. I feel like I'm getting fatter than before.

B Your metabolic rate* slows down. You have to eat less and move more*.

A I'll stop eating fatty food* and start exercising.

B You should maintain a healthy weight to stay fit*.

A 올해도 거의 절반이나 지났어.
B 나이 들수록 시간이 더 빨리 가는 것 같아.
A 맞아. 예전보다 살도 더 찌는 것 같아.
B 신진대사가 둔화되잖아. 덜 먹고 더 움직여야 해.
A 기름진 음식 그만 먹고 운동 시작할 거야.
B 건강하려면 적정 체중을 유지해야 해.

기타표현체크

- metabolic rate 신진대사율
- fatty food 기름진 음식
- eat less and move more 덜 먹고 더 움직이다
- stay fit 건강을 유지하다

❶ be halfway through sth 절반쯤 지나다(끝내다)

A We're already halfway through the week.

B Time flies. It will be the weekend before you know it.

A 벌써 일주일의 절반이 지났어.

B 시간 빠르네. 주말도 금방 올 거야.

❷ the 비교급 주어+동사, the 비교급 주어+동사
~할수록 ~하다

A Why do you donate even though you're not rich?

B The more you share, the happier you become.

A 부자도 아닌데 왜 기부하는 거니?

B 나눌수록 더 행복해지기 때문이지.

❸ get + 비교급+than before 예전보다 더 ~하다

A My kids are getting fatter than before these days.

B Today, obesity is a serious health problem.

A 요즘 아이들이 예전보다 더 뚱뚱해지고 있어.

B 오늘날 비만이 심각한 건강 문제야.

❹ maintain a healthy weight 적정 체중을 유지하다

A I've gained weight recently. I'm really out of shape.

B You should maintain a healthy weight to stay in shape.

A 최근에 체중이 늘었어. 몸매가 아주 엉망이야.

B 건강을 유지하려면 적정 체중을 유지해야 해.

다음 주어진 우리말을 영어로 말해 보세요.

01 이 근처에 갈 만한 데 있어?

----

02 별일 없지?

----

03 쉴 시간이 없어.

----

04 (힘든 상황) 어떻게 지내?

----

05 그럭저럭 지내.

----

06 얻은 게 있으면 잃는 게 있기 마련이지.

----

07 그들은 슬럼프에 빠진 것 같아.

----

08 올해도 거의 절반이나 지났어.

● 정답 01. Is there a good place to go around here? 02. Is everything okay? 03. I have no time for rest. 04. How are you holding up? 05. Just getting by. 06. There's always a trade off. 07. I guess they're in a slump. 08. We're almost halfway through the year.

DAY
051~055

MP3와 저자 강의를 들어 보세요.

DAY 051

내 시력 돌려줘

Day 051

MP3 강의 듣기

My eyesight got worse recently.

최근에 시력이 나빠졌어.

A I think my eyesight* got worse* recently.

B It comes with old age. My vision is blurry* at night.

A My goodness! That's what I've been afraid of.

B Go to the clinic to **get your eyes checked**.

A It's been **on my mind**, but I **haven't gotten around to** it.

B You **got your hands full** taking care of your kids*.

A 최근에 시력이 나빠진 것 같아.
B 노안이 온 거야. 나도 저녁에 눈이 침침해.
A 이런! 내가 늘 걱정했던 거야.
B 안과에 가서 검사 좀 해봐.
A 늘 생각은 했는데 시간을 못 냈어.
B 아이들 돌보느라 너무 바빴으니까.

기타표현체크

- eyesight   시력(vision)
- blurry   흐릿한

- get worse   악화되다
- take care of sb   ~를 돌보다

Mini Dialogues

① get sth checked 검사를 받다

A My teeth hurt badly. I think I have a cavity.

B That's terrible. You need to get them checked.

A 이가 많이 아파. 충치가 생겼나 봐.
B 저런. 검사를 좀 받아 봐야겠네.

② sth is[have sth]on one's mind ~가 마음에 걸리다

A You look blue. You have something on your mind?

B I think I have hurt my friend's feelings yesterday.

A 우울해 보이는데. 무슨 걱정거리 있어?
B 어제 내 친구의 감정을 상하게 한 것 같아.

③ haven't gotten around to sth ~할 시간을 못 내다

A Have you finished your new English novel?

B No. I haven't gotten around to reading it yet.

A 새로 구입한 영어 소설 다 읽었어?
B 아니. 아직 시간을 내지 못했어.

④ have[get] one's hands full -ing
~하느라 매우 바쁘다

A Where is the TV remote? I can't find it anywhere.

B Keep looking. I have my hands full cooking.

A TV 리모컨 어디 있어? 아무리 찾아도 없네.
B 계속 찾아봐. 나는 요리하느라 엄청 바빠.

🎧 Day 052

I could eat a horse.

MP3 강의 듣기

뭐든 다 먹을 수 있을 것 같아.

A **How's** your fishing **coming along?**

B I got a lot of bites, but mostly **came up empty-handed.**

A Let's **get ready to** cook. I'm so hungry **I could eat a horse.**

B I feel thirsty*. Where did you put the beers?

A They're in the blue cooler* next to the rock.

B We should set up the tent* before it gets dark*.

A 낚시는 잘 되어 가고 있어?
B 입질은 많았는데 대부분 허탕이야.
A 요리할 준비를 하자. 배고파 죽겠어.
B 목마르다. 맥주는 어디에다 뒀어?
A 바위 옆에 청색 아이스박스 안에 있어.
B 어두워지기 전에 텐트부터 쳐야겠다.

기타표현체크

- feel thirsty 목이 마르다
- set up the tent 텐트를 치다
- cooler 아이스박스
- get dark 어두워지다

❶ How is sth coming along? ~는 어떻게 되어 가?

A How is your new year's resolution coming along?
B So far so good. The problem is I'm getting lazy.

A 네 새해 다짐은 어떻게 되어 가고 있어?
B 지금까지는 좋아. 게을러지는 게 문제야.

❷ come (up) empty-handed 허탕을 치다, 빈손으로 오다

A Michell came empty-handed to my birthday party.
B That's ridiculous! Maybe she is out of her mind.

A 미셸이 내 생일 파티에 빈손으로 왔어.
B 말도 안 돼. 제정신이 아닌가 봐.

❸ get ready to + 동사원형 ~할 준비를 하다

A I have a good news. I have reached this year's goal.
B You're so amazing. Let's get ready to celebrate.

A 좋은 소식이 있어. 올해 목표를 달성했어.
B 정말 대단하다. 축하할 준비를 하자.

❹ I could eat a horse (배가 고파서) 뭐든 다 먹을 수 있을 것 같다

A I am so hungry that I could eat a horse.
B Hang on a second. I'll be right there.

A 배고파 죽을 것 같아요.
B 잠깐만. 금방 가져갈게.

DAY 053

How do you put up with it?

어떻게 참는 거야?

A Holy cow! What's up with* all the noise?

B It's the upstairs neighbors. I'll **bring it up with** them.

A It's dead serious. How do you **put up with** it?

B Besides* the noise, they're really good people.

A Are you **standing up for** them? You're really something*.

B **I can see where you're coming from.** That's how* you live in an apartment building.

A 이런! 이건 무슨 소음이야?
B 위층 이웃이야. 얘기 좀 해야겠다.
A 정말 심각하다. 저걸 어떻게 참니?
B 소음만 제외하면 정말 좋은 사람들이야.
A 그 사람들 편드는 거야? 정말 대단하다.
B 무슨 말인지 알아. 아파트에 사는 게 그래.

기타표현체크

• What's up with sb/sth   ~는 대체 뭐야?
• be really something   정말 대단하다
• besides sth   ~를 제외하고
• That's how 주어+동사   ~는 그런 거야

140

❶ bring it up with sb ~에게 (불편한) 말을 꺼내다

A We want it to be transparent about the actual costs.

B Everyone is reluctant to bring it up with the boss.

A 우리는 실제 비용이 얼마인지 투명하길 원해.

B 모두가 사장님에게 얘기 꺼내는 걸 싫어해.

❷ put up with sth ~을 견디다

A He is full of himself. He thinks of no one else.

B I hate him. I don't know how she puts up with him.

A 그는 거만해. 다른 사람은 안중에도 없어.

B 정말 싫어. 그녀가 어떻게 참는지 모르겠어.

❸ stand up for sb/sth ~을 옹호하다, 편들다

A I'll promise to pay you back if you take my side.

B Don't worry. I'll stand up for you no matter what.

A 네가 내 편을 들어준다면 보답을 약속할게.

B 걱정 마. 무슨 일이 있어도 널 지지할 거야.

❹ I can see where you're coming from
무슨 말인지 알아

A This pillow is a must-have item. You have to buy one.

B I can see where you're coming from. But I'm not sure.

A 이 베개는 필수품이야. 하나 구입해.

B 무슨 말인지 아는데. 난 잘 모르겠어.

DAY 054

사랑 싸움 그만해

Day 054

MP3 강의 듣기

We're history.

우린 완전히 끝났어.

A **How is it going with** your boyfriend?

B We broke up* last week after a big fight.

A Not again! *You guys will make up* in the end.

B We're history*. I have already **moved on**.

A Don't worry. There's a lid for every pot*.

B I**'ve had enough of** him **bossing me around**.

A 남자 친구와 어떻게 지내?
B 지난주에 크게 싸우고 헤어졌어.
A 또야? 결국 화해할 거잖아.
B 우린 끝났어. 이미 마음 정리했어.
A 걱정 마. 짚신도 다 짝이 있으니까.
B 나한테 잔소리하는 거 참을 만큼 참았어.

기타표현체크

- break up 헤어지다
- make up 화해하다
- There is a lid for every pot 짚신도 짝이 있다

- Not again! 또야!
- We are history 우린 끝났어

1 How is it going with sb/sth ~는 어떻게 되고 있어?

A How is it going with your business?
B It's been slow. I'm barely breaking even.

A 사업은 좀 어떠신가요?
B 안돼요. 현상 유지만 하고 있어요.

2 move on (to sth) ~로 넘어가다, 새로 시작하다

A I don't think we have any more questions.
B OK. Then let's move on to the next topic.

A 더 이상 질문이 없는 것 같은데요.
B 좋아요. 그럼 다음 주제로 넘어가죠.

3 have had enough of sb/sth ~을 더 이상 못 참다

A I have had enough of your stupid tricks.
B I know you won't fall for them. But it's fun.

A 네 유치한 속임수 진절머리 나.
B 너 안 속는 거 알아. 근데 재밌잖아.

4 boss sb around ~에게 잔소리하다

A You're not my boss. Stop bossing me around.
B I don't mean to bother you. I mean it.

A 넌 내 상사도 아니잖아. 잔소리하지 마.
B 널 귀찮게 하려는 건 아니야. 정말이야.

DAY 055

I haven't done it for ages.

해 본 지 정말 오래됐어.

A We finally got together*. Let's go bowling.

B I **suck at** bowling. I **haven't done it for ages.**

A **Don't be such a crybaby.** I'll **go easy on** you.

B I threw a bunch of gutter balls* last time.

A The losing team pays for the game*. OK?

B Good. Let's have a practice round* before we make teams*.

A 드디어 모였구나. 볼링 치러 가자.
B 나 볼링 못 쳐. 쳐 본 지 오래됐어.
A 엄살 좀 부리지 마. 살살 할게.
B 지난번에 도랑으로 엄청 빠졌어.
A 진 팀이 게임비 내는 거야. 어때?
B 좋아. 팀 나누기 전에 연습 경기부터 하자.

기타표현체크

- get together 만나다, 모이다
- pay for the game 게임비를 내다
- make teams 팀을 나누다
- threw a gutter ball 도랑으로 빠뜨리다
- have a practice round 연습 경기를 하다

1 suck at sth ~를 정말 못하다

A You're a big fan of basketball. Let's play in the gym.

B I like watching sports, but I really suck at playing them.

A 농구 진짜 좋아하는구나. 체육관에서 한 게임 하자.

B 난 스포츠 보는 건 좋아하지만 하는 건 정말 못해.

2 haven't done sth for ages ~ 안 한 지 오래되었다

A The bathroom is dirty. When did you last clean it?

B I'm so sorry. I haven't done any cleaning for ages.

A 화장실이 더러워. 언제 마지막으로 청소했어?

B 정말 미안해. 청소 안 한 지 진짜 오래됐어.

3 Don't be such a crybaby 엄살 피우지 마

A I think I blew my English test. It was too difficult.

B You're crying wolf again. Don't be such a crybaby.

A 영어 시험 완전 망친 것 같아. 너무 어려웠어.

B 또 거짓말하고 있네. 엄살 좀 피우지 마.

4 go easy on sb ~에게 살살 하다, 봐 주다

A Do you want to play table tennis? We'll play doubles.

B Fasten your seat belts! I won't go easy on you this time.

A 탁구 칠래? 복식으로 할 거야.

B 긴장하는 게 좋을 거야. 이번엔 안 봐 줄 거야.

다음 주어진 우리말을 영어로 말해 보세요.

01 최근에 시력이 나빠졌어.

----

02 나도 저녁에 눈이 침침해.

----

03 맥주는 어디에다 뒀어?

----

04 뭐든 다 먹을 수 있을 것 같아.

----

05 그 사람들 옹호하는 거야?

----

06 짚신도 다 짝이 있으니까.

----

07 해 본 지 정말 오래됐어.

----

08 연습 경기 하자.

●정답 01. My eyesight got worse recently.　02. My vision is blurry at night.　03. Where did you put the beers?　04. I could eat a horse.　05. Are you standing up for them?　06. There's a lid for every pot.　07. I haven't done it for ages.　08. Let's have a practice round.

DAY
056~060

MP3와 저자 강의를 들어 보세요.

초보 탈출!

 Day 056

DAY 056
It bothers me that my face breaks out.

MP3 강의 듣기

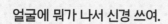

얼굴에 뭐가 나서 신경 쓰여.

A It bothers me that my face breaks out*.

B What do you say to* getting a facial on Saturday?

A Sounds great!* What time shall we meet?*

B Let's meet at 2 o'clock. How does that sound?

A Good! By the way, how much does it cost?

B It won't cost you a lot of money.

A 얼굴에 뭐가 나서 신경 쓰여.
B 토요일에 얼굴 마사지 받으러 갈래?
A 그거 좋지. 몇 시에 만날까?
B 2시 정각에 만나자. 어때?
A 좋아. 근데 비용은 얼마나 들어?
B 돈이 많이 들지 않을 거야.

기타표현체크

• break out (피부) 트러블이 생기다
• (That) sounds great 그거 좋지

• What do you say to -ing? ~하는 건 어때?
• What time shall we meet? 몇 시에 만날까?

❶ It bothers me that 주어+동사 ~가 마음에 걸리다

A It seems that my son is getting to school on time.
B But it still bothers me he's not getting used to it.

A 아들이 학교에 제시간에 가는 것 같아.
B 근데 적응을 못하는 게 아직 마음에 걸려.

❷ get a facial 얼굴 마사지를 받다

A You have nice skin. Do you get a facial regularly?
B Come on. You should see me without makeup.

A 피부가 좋은데 정기적으로 얼굴 마사지 받니?
B 말도 안 돼. 화장 안 한 얼굴을 봐야겠구나.

❸ How does sth sound? ~는 어때?

A Let's have lunch next Monday. How does it sound?
B Let me check my schedule. That would be fine.

A 다음 주 월요일에 점심 먹자. 어때?
B 일정 좀 확인해 볼게. 괜찮을 것 같아.

❹ cost sb a lot of money 돈이 많이 들다

A Did you get your car back from the body shop?
B Yes, but it cost me a lot of money to get it repaired.

A 정비소에서 네 자동차 찾았어?
B 응. 근데 수리비가 너무 많이 들었어.

DAY 057

노후에 뭘 할까

🎧 Day 057

MP3 강의 듣기

Where do you see yourself in 10 years?

10년 후에는 뭘 하고 있을 것 같아?

A **Where do you see yourself** in 10 years?

B I'm not sure, but I'll be still working here.

A I want to **start my own business** around* 50.

B It's tough to **start from scratch** again.

A I'd like to run a small restaurant* sometime.

B Awesome! I**'m jealous of** people with dreams.

A 10년 후에 뭘 하고 있을 것 같아?
B 잘 모르겠지만 여기서 일하고 있겠지.
A 난 50살 정도가 되면 사업을 시작하고 싶어.
B 처음부터 다시 시작하는 게 어렵지.
A 언젠가는 조그만 식당을 운영하고 싶어.
B 멋진데! 난 꿈이 있는 사람들이 부럽더라.

기타표현체크

• in 10 years (지금부터) 10년 후에   • around 50   50살 무렵에
• run a restaurant   식당을 운영하다

150

① Where do you see yourself? (미래에) 어떤 모습일 것 같아?

A Where do you see yourself 5 years from now?

B I will be running a company. I'm working hard for it.

A 지금부터 5년 후에 넌 뭘 하고 있을 것 같아?
B 회사를 경영하고 있겠지. 열심히 준비 중이야.

② start one's (own) business (자신의) 사업을 시작하다

A Do you have something in mind for your future?

B Yes, I'm going to start my own business sooner or later.

A 미래를 위해 생각해 두신 게 있나요?
B 네. 조만간 개인 사업을 시작하려고요.

③ start (sth) from scratch 처음부터 시작하다

A I'm not able to get into college with this score.

B You should start your study from scratch.

A 이 점수로 대학에 입학 못할 것 같아.
B 넌 공부를 처음부터 다시 시작해야 해.

④ be jealous of sb ~를 부러워하다

A I'm jealous of your slim figure. Tell me your secret.

B Don't eat too much and do some cardio exercise.

A 네 날씬한 몸매가 부러워. 비법 좀 알려 줘.
B 과식하지 말고 유산소 운동을 해.

DAY 058

Did you walk the dog?

강아지 산책시켰어?

MP3 강의 듣기

A Did you **walk the dog** this morning?

B No. I'm **taking her to the vet*** for grooming*.

A She needs to get a vaccination* this time.

B By the way, I can't seem to find her leash*.

A I **took** it **out of** my car for sure yesterday.

B I'll look for it after **putting on my makeup.**

A 오늘 아침에 강아지 산책시켰어?
B 아니. 동물 병원 가서 털 손질 시키려고.
A 이번에는 예방 접종도 받아야 해.
B 그런데 목줄을 찾을 수가 없네.
A 어제 차에서 분명히 꺼냈는데.
B 화장하고 나서 내가 찾아볼게.

기타표현체크

- vet (veterinary clinic) 동물 병원
- get a vaccination 예방 접종을 하다
- grooming (동물의) 털 손질
- leash 목줄

① walk the dog 개를 산책시키다

A I'll be a little late today. I have plans with James.
B Have a good time. I'm walking the dog now.

A 오늘 좀 늦을 거야. 제임스와 약속이 있어.
B 좋은 시간 보내. 강아지 산책 중이야.

② take one's pet to the vet ~을 동물 병원에 데려가다

A Today I'm taking my cat to the vet to get vaccinated.
B Come to think of it, I need to have my dog groomed.

A 오늘 우리 고양이 예방 접종을 하러 동물 병원에 갈 거야.
B 그러고 보니, 우리 강아지 털 손질 시켜야 하는데.

③ take A out of B A를 B에서 꺼내다

A It's starting to rain. I didn't bring my umbrella.
B I have two. I'll take one out of my car.

A 비가 오기 시작하네. 우산 안 가져왔는데.
B 나한테 두 개 있어. 차에서 하나 꺼내 올게.

④ put on (one's) makeup 화장을 하다

A You spend much time putting on makeup.
B Because I want to cover my skin problems.

A 화장하는 데 많은 시간을 쓰는구나.
B 피부 트러블이 안 보이게 하고 싶어서.

MP3 강의 듣기

DAY 059

Just get to the point.

그냥 요점만 말해.

A I don't know how to put it into words*.

B I've got a bad feeling*. Just get to the point*.

A I guess this is it*. We are so different.

B I think we need to relax and **take it slow.**

A I've **given it a lot of thought.** I've **run out of patience.**

B We've been great together. Please **think it over.**

A 어떻게 말해야 할지 모르겠다.
B 느낌이 안 좋은데. 요점만 말해.
A 이게 끝인가 봐. 우린 너무 달라.
B 진정하고 천천히 생각해 보자.
A 많이 생각했어. 인내심이 바닥났어.
B 그동안 좋았잖아. 다시 생각해 봐.

기타표현체크

• put sth into words 말로 표현하다
• get to the point 요점만 말하다
• have(get) a bad feeling 느낌이 안 좋다
• I guess this is it 이게 끝인가 봐

❶ take it slow (신중하게) 천천히 하다

A When are you getting married? You shouldn't put it off.

B I want to take it slow until I find someone right for me.

A 언제 결혼할 거야? 미루면 안 되잖아.

B 나와 맞는 사람을 찾을 때까지 천천히 찾으려고.

---

❷ give it a lot of thought 많이 생각하다

A Let's move to a big city for our children's education?

B Have you given it a lot of thought before you said it?

A 아이들 교육을 위해 큰 도시로 이사 가자.

B 얘기하기 전에 많이 생각해 본 거야?

---

❸ run out of patience 인내심이 바닥나다

A The dog keeps barking. What's wrong with the owner?

B I can't take it anymore. I've run out of patience.

A 개가 계속 짖네. 주인은 대체 뭐하는 거야?

B 더 이상 못 참겠어. 인내심이 바닥났어.

---

❹ think sth over 곰곰이 생각하다

A Honey, why don't we visit grandpa this weekend?

B I don't feel like going out, but I'll think it over.

A 자기야, 주말에 할아버지 댁에 방문할까?

B 외출하고 싶지 않은데, 생각 좀 해 볼게.

🎧 Day 060

DAY 060

Don't look a gift horse in the mouth.

MP3 강의 듣기

선물에 트집 잡는 거 아니야.

A **Can I talk to you for a second?**

B Sure. You **have something up your sleeve?**

A I've got two tickets to* a concert. Are you in?*

B Are they R seats? I want to sit in the front.*

A Hey, don't **look a gift horse in the mouth.**

B That's true*. **Beggars can't be choosers.**

A 잠깐 얘기 좀 할 수 있어?

B 물론. 뭐 특별한 거라도 있어?

A 콘서트 티켓이 두 장 있어. 같이 갈래?

B R석이야? 앞쪽에 앉고 싶은데.

A 이봐. 선물에 트집 잡는 거 아니야.

B 그건 그래. 가릴 처지가 아니지.

기타표현체크

• a ticket to sth ~ 가는 티켓
• sit in the front 앞쪽에 앉다

• Are you in? 같이 갈래?
• That's true 그건 그래

① Can I talk to you for a second? 얘기 좀 할까?

A Got a minute? Can I talk to you for a second?

B Sure. Have a seat. What do you need?

A 시간 좀 돼? 잠깐 얘기 좀 할 수 있어?
B 그럼. 여기 앉아. 뭐 필요한 거 있어?

② have(get) something up one's sleeve
(숨겨둔) 뭔가가 있다

A You've got something up your sleeve. Spit it out.

B I'm not supposed to tell anyone. Mum's the word.

A 너 뭔가 숨기는 거 있구나. 말해 봐.
B 아무한테도 말하면 안 돼. 비밀이야.

③ look a gift horse in the mouth 선물에 트집 잡다

A My mom bought me a new bag. But it's too tacky.

B You should grow up. Don't look a gift horse in the mouth.

A 엄마가 새 가방을 사줬는데 너무 촌스러워.
B 철 좀 들어라. 선물에 불평하지 마.

④ beggars can't be choosers
(찬 밥 더운 밥) 가릴 처지가 아니다

A I got some bread for you. It just came out of the oven.

B I don't like the bread, but beggars can't be choosers.

A 너 주려고 빵 좀 사 왔어. 방금 구운 거야.
B 빵은 안 좋아하지만 가릴 처지가 아니지.

다음 주어진 우리말을 영어로 말해 보세요.

01 몇 시에 만날까?

----

02 처음부터 다시 시작하는 것이 어렵지.

----

03 조그만 식당을 운영하고 싶어.

----

04 강아지 산책시켰어?

----

05 그냥 요점만 말해.

----

06 인내심이 바닥났어.

----

07 앞쪽에 앉고 싶은데.

----

08 찬 밥 더운 밥 가리면 안 되지.

●정답 01.What time shall we meet? 02. It's tough to start from scratch again. 03. I'd like to run a small restaurant. 04. Did you walk the dog this morning? 05. Just get to the point. 06. I've run out of patience. 07. I want to sit in the front. 08. Beggars can't be choosers.

DAY
061~065

MP3와 저자 강의를 들어 보세요.

이른 출장

I slept through the alarm.

MP3 강의 듣기

알람 소리를 못 듣고 잤어.

A Sorry I'm late. I **slept through the alarm**.

B You must **be exhausted from** the after-party*.

A It's freezing in here. Can you turn on the heater*?

B Alright. Let me **put on some music.**

A Thanks. I'll **wake myself up with** some **coffee**.

B Just stay put*. I'll go get some coffee*.

A 늦어서 미안해. 알람 소리를 못 듣고 잤어.
B 뒤풀이 때문에 많이 피곤했구나.
A 엄청 춥다. 히터 좀 틀어 줄래?
B 알았어. 음악도 틀어 줄게.
A 고마워. 커피 마시고 정신 좀 차려야지.
B 여기 있어 봐. 가서 커피 사 올게.

기타표현체크

- after-party 뒤풀이
- stay put 그대로 있다
- turn on the heater 히터를 틀다
- get some coffee 커피를 사 오다

❶ sleep through the alarm 알람 소리를 못 듣고 자다

A Why did you skip your swimming lesson this morning?
B I'm sorry. I was so tired that I slept through the alarm.

A 왜 오늘 아침에 수영 강습 안 나왔어?
B 미안. 너무 피곤해서 알람 소리를 못 들었어.

❷ be exhausted from sth ~로 녹초가 되다

A I'm exhausted from the heat. I'm sweating a lot.
B I'll crank up the air conditioner. You want some iced tea?

A 더위에 정말 지친다. 땀이 줄줄 흐르네.
B 에어컨 세게 틀어 줄게. 아이스티 한잔 줄까?

❸ put[turn] on some music 음악(노래)을 틀다

A Check this out. I got a new bluetooth speaker.
B Let's turn down the lights and put on some music.

A 이거 봐. 새 블루투스 스피커 구입했어.
B 조명을 낮추고 음악 틀어 보자.

❹ wake oneself up with coffee
커피 마시고 정신 차리다

A Are you OK? If you're sleepy, I'll take the wheel.
B It's okay. I'll wake myself up with some coffee.

A 괜찮아요? 당신 졸리면 제가 운전할게요
B 아직 괜찮아. 커피 마시고 정신 좀 차릴게.

DAY 062

기계치 친구

Day 062

MP3 강의 듣기

Technology has come a long way.

기술 정말 좋아졌다.

A Can you tell me how to **save** this **onto** the phone?

B **Log onto the Internet** and push this button.

A Technology has **come a long way**. I'm just old school*.

B You should keep up with* the latest technology to survive.

A You **touch a sore spot** every time you say that.

B I'm sorry, but I didn't mean it*.

A 이거 휴대폰에 저장하는 법 좀 알려 줄래?
B 인터넷에 접속해서 이 버튼을 눌러 봐.
A 기술 정말 좋아졌다. 난 구식인가 봐.
B 생존하려면 최신 기술을 따라가야지.
A 말할 때마다 아픈 곳을 건드리네.
B 미안해. 일부러 그런 건 아니야.

기타표현체크

· **old school** 구식인, 구닥다리인
· **I didn't mean it** 그런 뜻은 아니었어
· **keep up with sth** (기술, 트렌드) ~를 따라가다

1 save A onto B A를 B에 저장하다

A You should not open emails from unknown senders.
B They want you to save malware onto your PC.

A 출처가 불분명한 이메일을 열람해서는 안 돼.
B 컴퓨터에 악성코드를 설치하려고 하는 거야.

2 log onto the Internet 인터넷에 접속하다

A Is there any way to take online classes at home?
B Sure. I'll demonstrate how to log onto the Internet.

A 집에서 온라인 강좌를 들을 수 있는 방법이 있을까?
B 물론이지. 인터넷에 접속하는 방법을 가르쳐 줄게.

3 come a long way 많은 발전을 하다; 성장하다

A Mom, what do you think of my swimming?
B You've come a long way. I was impressed.

A 엄마, 제 수영 실력 어때요?
B 많이 발전했구나. 인상적이었어.

4 touch a sore spot 아픈 곳(약점)을 건드리다

A My mother passed away. I still miss her very much.
B I'm so sorry. I seem to have touched a sore spot.

A 어머니는 돌아가셨어요. 아직도 많이 보고 싶어요.
B 정말 미안해요. 제가 아픈 곳을 건드린 것 같네요.

163

DAY 063

He picks on every little detail.

사사건건 트집을 잡아.

A You look depressed. What's wrong?*

B It's my boss. He **picks on** every little detail.

A I think he **mixes business with pleasure**.

B He's such a control freak*. I want to **submit my resignation.**

A Take it down a notch*. Let's **get to the bottom of** this.

B We don't need to. I'll just do what I'm told*.

A 우울해 보이네. 무슨 일이야?
B 부장님 때문에. 사사건건 트집을 잡아.
A 공과 사를 구별 못 하시는 것 같아.
B 뭐든 자기 맘대로야. 사표 쓰고 싶다.
A 진정해. 함께 원인을 밝혀 보자.
B 그럴 필요 없어. 시킨 대로 할래.

기타표현체크

- What's wrong? 무슨 일 있어?
- take it down a notch 진정하다
- control freak 통제광(자기 맘대로 하려는 사람)
- do what[as] I'm told 시키는 대로 하다

① pick on sb/sth ~를 괴롭히다, ~을 트집 잡다

A I don't get it. Why does he keep picking on me?
B Maybe he's interested in you. He's flirting with you.

A 이해가 안 돼. 왜 그가 계속 날 괴롭히는 거지?
B 너한테 관심 있는 거 같은데. 집적거리는 거야.

② mix business with pleasure 공과 사를 혼동하다

A Don't take that attitude. You need to be flexible.
B I'm sorry, but I don't mix business with pleasure.

A 너무 뻣뻣하게 굴지 마. 융통성이 있어야지.
B 미안한데, 난 공과 사를 혼동하지 않거든.

③ submit one's resignation 사직서를 제출하다

A I think you're straining yourself with two jobs.
B So I've decided to submit my resignation soon.

A 넌 두 가지 일을 하느라 너무 무리하는 것 같아.
B 그래서 조만간 사직서를 제출하기로 결심했어.

④ get to the bottom of sth ~의 원인을 밝혀내다

A I heard he was fired. I don't know what's going on.
B It smells fishy. We should get to the bottom of this.

A 그가 해고되었다면서. 무슨 일인지 모르겠네.
B 수상한데. 이 문제의 진상을 규명해야 해.

사랑도 노력이야

🎧 Day 064

MP3 강의 듣기

She has the seven-year itch.

그녀는 권태기야.

A How is Helen? I **haven't heard** anything **since** her wedding.

B She's doing okay. Except that she **had a falling-out with** her husband a few times.

A They were a lovey-dovey couple* back in college*.

B Looks like* she **has the seven-year itch**.

A It **takes a lot of effort** to maintain a marriage*.

B Absolutely*! I really want them to be happy.

A 헬렌은 어때? 결혼 후에 소식을 못 들었어.
B 잘 지내. 남편하고 몇 번 크게 다툰 것 빼고.
A 두 사람 대학 때 닭살 커플이었잖아.
B 그녀가 권태기인 것 같은데.
A 결혼 생활에도 많은 노력이 필요해.
B 당연하지! 걔네들 정말 행복하면 좋겠어.

기타표현체크

• lovey-dovey couple 닭살 커플
• Looks like 주어+동사 ~인 것 같다
• back in college 대학 다닐 때
• maintain a marriage 결혼 생활을 유지하다

Mini Dialogues

1 현재완료 + since + 과거 시제 ~이후로 ~하지 못했다

A Do I have to learn English? I'm not improving.
B Right. I have been learning it since I was 10 years old.

A 영어를 꼭 배워야 해? 실력이 늘지 않아.
B 맞아. 10살 때부터 지금까지 배우고 있어.

2 have a falling-out (with sb) ~와 사이가 틀어지다

A I think I haven't seen you with Tom lately.
B We had a falling-out. I don't want to talk about it.

A 요즘 네가 톰이랑 어울리는 걸 못 본 것 같아.
B 심하게 다퉜어. 그 얘기는 하고 싶지 않아.

3 have(get) the seven-year itch 권태기를 겪다

A He is weird. He makes a fuss over nothing.
B He's got the seven-year itch. He's different from before.

A 그가 이상해. 별거 아닌 일로 난리야.
B 권태기가 왔나 봐. 예전과 달라졌어.

4 take a lot of effort 많은 노력이 요구되다

A It takes a lot of effort to raise kids.
B But it's fulfilling. Kids give us a lot of joy.

A 아이들 키우는 건 많은 노력이 필요해.
B 하지만 보람 있어. 많은 기쁨을 주잖아.

It's better than nothing.

안 하는 것보단 낫지.

A Nice weather. Fall is just around the corner*.

B Look at the clouds. **It's a perfect day** for a picnic.

A Shall we go for a walk* after lunch?

B Definitely. I **barely had time to** exercise lately.

A Just 30 minutes a day works*. It's **better than nothing.**

B Oh, my! I **lost track of time.** Let's get back to work*.

A 날씨 좋다. 가을이 성큼 다가왔어.
B 구름 좀 봐. 소풍 가기 딱 좋은 날씨야.
A 점심 먹고 나서 산책할래?
B 물론이지. 요즘 운동할 시간이 거의 없었어.
A 하루 30분도 효과가 있어. 안 하는 것보단 낫지.
B 어머나. 시간 가는 줄 몰랐네. 일하러 가자.

기타표현체크

• sth is around the corner (~이) 가까이 있다
• work 효과가 있다
• go for a walk 산책하다
• get back to work 업무에 복귀하다

① It's a perfect day (for+명사 / to+동사원형)
~하기 좋은 날이다

A Nice weather! It's a perfect day for a drive.
B Let's go out to the Han River to get some air.

A 날씨 좋은데! 드라이브하기 좋은 날이야.
B 한강에 가서 바람이나 쐬자.

② barely have time to+동사원형 ~할 틈도 없다

A How was your weekend? You look tired.
B I was so busy that I barely had time to breathe.

A 주말 잘 보냈어? 너 피곤해 보인다.
B 너무 바빠서 숨 돌릴 틈도 없었어.

③ (Sth is) better than nothing 없는 것보단 낫지

A I can't play games because your computer is too slow.
B Better than nothing. Plus, I don't like computer games.

A 네 컴퓨터는 너무 느려서 게임을 할 수가 없어.
B 없는 것보단 낫지. 그리고 난 게임 안 좋아해.

④ lose track of time 시간 가는 줄 모르다

A Why were you so late? I was worried about you.
B Sorry. I lost track of time while I was bowling.

A 왜 이렇게 늦었어. 걱정 많이 했잖아.
B 미안해. 볼링 치느라 시간 가는 줄 몰랐어.

다음 주어진 우리말을 영어로 말해 보세요.

01 알람 소리를 못 듣고 잤어.

----

02 커피 마시고 정신 좀 차려야지.

----

03 난 구식인가 봐.

----

04 그런 뜻은 아니었어.

----

05 사표 쓰고 싶다.

----

06 함께 원인을 밝혀 보자.

----

07 결혼 생활에도 많은 노력이 필요해.

----

08 시간 가는 줄 몰랐네.

●정답 01. I slept through the alarm. 02. I'll wake myself up with some coffee. 03. I'm just old school. 04. I didn't mean it. 05. I want to submit my resignation. 06. Let's get to the bottom of this. 07. It takes a lot of effort to maintain a marriage. 08. I lost track of time.

DAY
066~070

MP3와 저자 강의를 들어 보세요.

DAY 066

It's time to get on the bus.

버스에 탑승할 시간이야.

A Seems like* the bus is running late because of heavy snow.

B Yeah. It should've been here 20 minutes ago.

A Let me go to the restroom real quick.

B Take your time*. I'll be in the convenience store*.

A I'm back. It's time to get on the bus.

B Have a safe trip. Text me* when you arrive.

A 폭설 때문에 버스가 늦어지나 봐.
B 그러게. 20분 전에 도착했어야 하는데.
A 화장실 좀 얼른 다녀올게.
B 천천히 다녀와. 편의점에 있을게.
A 나 왔어. 탑승할 시간이다.
B 잘 다녀와. 도착하면 문자 보내.

기타표현체크

- Seems like 주어+동사　～인 것 같다
- convenience store　편의점
- take one's time　천천히 ～하다
- text sb　～에게 문자를 보내다

① run late because of sth ~ 때문에 늦어지다

A The bus is running late because of the traffic jam.

B I'm so annoyed. It should've been here 20 minutes ago.

A 교통 체증 때문에 버스가 늦어지고 있어.
B 짜증 나. 20분 전에 도착했어야 하는데.

② should have +과거분사 ~ 했어야 했다

A I should've listened to your advice back then.

B You're all grown up. Anyone can make a mistake.

A 그때 네 충고를 들었어야 했는데.
B 철들었네. 누구나 실수는 하는 거야.

③ 동사+ real quick 금방 ~하다

A I want to ask you something real quick. No pressure.

B Don't tell me you need to borrow some money.

A 간단히 뭐 물어볼게. 부담 안 가져도 돼.
B 설마 돈 빌려 달라고 하려는 건 아니겠지.

④ get on the bus / get in the taxi (버스/택시)를 타다

A There's a taxi coming. You can take this one.

B No. I can take the bus. Get in the taxi, quick!

A 저기 택시 온다. 이번 차 타고 가.
B 아니야. 난 버스 탈래. 너 얼른 타.

MP3 강의 듣기

DAY 067

You don't seem to know your place.

주제 파악을 못 하는 것 같은데.

A I **had a big fight** with my girlfriend yesterday.

B You guys used to **hit it off** when going out*.

A I'm tired of* her constant nagging.

B You don't seem to **know your place.**

A That's the truth*. She's too good for* me.

B **Be gentle with** her. She's the only one for you.

A 어제 여자 친구랑 크게 싸웠어.
B 너희들 사귈 때는 사이좋았잖아.
A 그녀의 끊임없는 잔소리에 질렸어.
B 너 주제 파악을 못 하는 것 같다.
A 그건 사실이야. 나한테 과분하지.
B 그녀에게 잘해. 너에겐 그녀밖에 없어.

기타표현체크

• go out (with sb) ~와 사귀다, 데이트하다
• That's the truth 정말이야
• be tired of sth/sb ~에 싫증 나다
• A is too good for B A는 B에게 과분하다

174

❶ have a big fight 크게 싸우다

A I had a big fight with my mom yesterday.

B Why don't you make up before it's too late?

A 어제 엄마와 크게 다퉜어.

B 너무 늦기 전에 화해하는 게 어때?

❷ hit it off (with sb) ~와 죽이 잘 맞다

A Your boss pokes his nose into everything.

B I don't think I can hit it off with him.

A 너희 부장님은 모든 일에 참견을 해.

B 그 분과 친하게 지내지 못할 것 같네.

❸ know one's place 주제 파악을 하다, 분수를 알다

A I'll raise your allowance if you study hard.

B I know my place. Don't get your hopes up.

A 공부 열심히 하면 용돈을 올려 줄게.

B 제 주제를 알죠. 너무 기대하진 마세요.

❹ be gentle with sb/sth ~에게 잘해 주다(부드럽게 대하다)

A Your husband is gentle with you. He's so sweet.

B I know. But I want him to cut back on smoking.

A 남편이 잘해 주네. 정말 자상한 사람이야.

B 그래. 하지만 그가 담배 좀 줄이면 좋겠어.

DAY 068

MP3 강의 듣기

Show them what you've got.

네 능력을 보여 줘.

A Are you ready for the job interview?

B No. I'm about to* **have a nervous breakdown.**

A Don't be so nervous. Everything will come up roses.

B I'll give it my best shot* and forget the rest*.

A Exactly! Show them what you've got*.

B Don't put pressure on me. I want to get it over with.

A 면접 준비는 다 했어?
B 아니. 신경 쇠약에 걸릴 것 같아.
A 너무 긴장하지 마. 다 잘 될 거야.
B 최선을 다하고 나머지는 잊을 거야.
A 바로 그거야! 네 능력을 보여 줘.
B 부담 주지 마. 빨리 해치우고 싶다.

기타표현체크

• be about to+동사원형   막 ~하려고 하다
• forget the rest   나머지는 잊다

• give it one's best shot   최선을 다하다
• show sb what you've got   ~에게 실력을 보여줘

① have a nervous breakdown 신경 쇠약에 걸리다

A I think you have been under a lot of stress lately.
B Right. I'm gonna have a nervous breakdown.

A 너 요즘 스트레스 많이 받는 것 같아.
B 그래. 신경 쇠약에 걸릴 것 같아.

② Everything comes up roses
모든 일이 잘 풀리다

A You've been in a good mood the last few days.
B You bet! Because everything is coming up roses.

A 너 최근 며칠 기분이 좋구나.
B 물론이지. 모든 일이 잘 되고 있어.

③ put (a lot of) pressure on sb
~에게 (많은) 부담을 주다

A I strongly believe you can somehow achieve it.
B Don't put pressure on me. It makes me more nervous.

A 네가 어떻게든 해 낼 거라고 굳게 믿어.
B 부담 주지 마. 그 말 들으니 더 떨린다.

④ get sth over with (하기 싫은 일을) 빨리 끝내다

A Are you done with your homework for today?
B Not yet. I'll get it over with as soon as possible.

A 오늘 꺼 숙제 다 했니?
B 아직요. 최대한 빨리 끝낼게요.

DAY 069

아기 재우기

🎧 Day 069

MP3 강의 듣기

He fell fast asleep.

곤히 잠들었어.

A Honey, did you put the baby to sleep?

B Yes. He fell fast asleep as soon as he lay down*.

A Maybe he didn't get enough sleep* today.

B Check if he sleeps on his stomach later.

A I'll check it when it's time to change his diaper*.

B I'm off work* tomorrow. I'll stay in bed until the last minute.

A 여보, 당신이 아기 재웠어?
B 응. 눕자마자 곯아떨어졌어.
A 오늘 잠을 충분히 못 잤을 거야.
B 나중에 엎드려 자는지 확인해 줘.
A 기저귀 갈 때 확인해 볼게.
B 내일 쉬는 날이야. 늦잠이나 자야지.

기타표현체크

* lie down   눕다
* change one's diaper   기저귀를 갈다
* get enough sleep   잠을 충분히 자다
* be off work   출근 안 하고 쉬다

178

① put sb to sleep 잠을 재우다; 지루하다

A How do you put your kids to sleep?

B I read storybooks and sing a lullaby.

A 넌 아이들 잘 때 어떻게 재워?

B 동화책 읽어 주고 자장가도 불러 주지.

② fall fast asleep 곤히 잠들다

A Did you get a good night's sleep last night?

B I fell fast asleep as soon as my head hit the pillow.

A 어젯밤에 잘 잤어?

B 머리를 대자마자 곯아떨어졌어.

③ sleep on one's stomach 엎드려 자다

A You should lie on your back. It's not good for your health.

B It's comfortable for me to sleep on my stomach.

A 똑바로 누워. 건강에 좋지 않아.

B 저는 엎드려서 자는 게 편해요.

④ stay in bed until the last minute
최대한 늦게 일어나다

A I'm having trouble waking up my son every day.

B He wants to stay in bed until the last minute.

A 매일 아들 녀석 깨우느라 힘들어.

B 최대한 늦게 일어나고 싶은 거지.

We go way back.

오래전부터 알고 지냈어.

A Mom, how do you know my teacher?

B We **go way back**. We **went to the same** high school.

A What a coincidence!* Were you close to* each other?

B Sure. We used to **be stuck at home** studying.

A Studying is not my thing*. I love hanging out*.

B That's fine. **To each their own.**

A 엄마, 우리 선생님 어떻게 아세요?
B 안 지 오래됐지. 고등학교 동창이야.
A 이런 우연이! 서로 친하셨어요?
B 물론이지. 집에 틀어박혀서 공부했지.
A 전 공부랑 안 맞아요. 노는 게 좋아요.
B 괜찮아. 취향은 각자 다른 거야.

기타표현체크

• What a coincidence! 이런 우연이 있다니!
• sth is not my thing ~는 나랑 안 맞다
• be close to sb ~와 친하다
• hang out (with sb) ~와 놀다, 어울리다

Mini Dialogues

❶ go way back 오래전부터 알고 지내다

A Since when did you know my grandfather?

B We go way back. We served in the military together.

A 언제부터 우리 할아버지를 알고 계셨나요?
B 오래전부터 알았지. 군대에서 함께 복무했어.

❷ went to the same + 학교 고등(대)학교 동창이다

A Your mother and I went to the same college.

B No wonder you were so close to each other.

A 너희 엄마랑 난 대학교 동창이야.
B 어쩐지 두 분이 되게 친하시더라.

❸ be stuck at home -ing 집에 틀어박혀 ~을 하다

A What are you doing this weekend? I'll go fishing.

B I'm going to be stuck at home doing some chores.

A 이번 주말에 뭐 할 거야? 난 낚시 갈 건데.
B 집에 틀어박혀서 집안일 좀 할 거야.

❹ to each their own 취향은 각자 다른 거니까

A I think playing computer games is a waste of time.

B Well, let's agree to disagree. To each their own.

A 컴퓨터 게임하는 건 시간 낭비라고 생각해.
B 서로 다르다는 걸 인정하자. 취향은 다르니까.

다음 주어진 우리말을 영어로 말해 보세요.

01 탑승할 시간이다.

----

02 도착하면 문자 보내.

----

03 그녀는 나한테 과분하지.

----

04 다 잘 될 거야.

----

05 부담 주지 마.

----

06 그는 곤히 잠들었어.

----

07 내일 쉬는 날이야.

----

08 오래전부터 알고 지냈어.

●정답 01. It's time to get on the bus.   02. Text me when you arrive.   03. She's too good for me.   04. Everything will come up roses.   05. Don't put pressure on me.   06. He fell fast asleep.   07. I'm off work tomorrow.   08. We go way back.

DAY
071~075

MP3와 저자 강의를 들어 보세요.

I'm having a bad hair day.

일진이 안 좋아.

A It's really coming down*. I'm **having a bad hair day.**

B Your luck **has nothing to do with** the weather.

A One day I **got caught in the rain** and **came down with** a cold.

B That's why you're not happy about* rainy days.

A Like they say, when it rains, it pours*.

B Calm down. Your're such a worrywart*.

A 비가 엄청 오네. 오늘 일진이 사납겠군.
B 운하고 날씨는 아무 상관없어.
A 언젠가 비를 맞고 감기에 걸렸거든.
B 그래서 비 오는 날을 안 좋아하는구나.
A 엎친 데 덮친다는 말이 있잖아.
B 진정해. 사서 걱정하지 말고.

기타표현체크

- It's coming down (비, 눈) 등이 억수같이 내리다 • be not happy about sth ~에 대해 기분이 안 좋다
- When it rains, it pours 엎친 데 덮치다 • worrywart 사소한 걱정을 하는 사람

① have a bad hair day 일진이 사납다

A I dropped my cell phone. I'm having a bad hair day.
B Never mind. It could happen at any time.

A 휴대폰을 떨어뜨렸어. 오늘 일진이 사납겠군.
B 신경 쓰지 마. 언제든 있는 일이야.

② have nothing to do with sth ~와 전혀 관계가 없다

A You're good at drawing. Did you go to art college?
B I just do it for fun. It has nothing to do with my major.

A 그림을 잘 그리네요. 미술 대학 나오셨어요?
B 그냥 재미로 해요. 전공하고 관계가 없어요.

③ get caught in the rain 비를 맞다

A How did you get home without an umbrella?
B I got caught in the rain on my way back home.

A 우산도 없이 집에 어떻게 도착했어?
B 집에 오는 도중에 비를 맞았어.

④ come down with + 병명 ~에 걸리다

A I feel chilly. I think I'm coming down with a cold.
B Be careful not to get sick from the air conditioning.

A 으슬으슬하네. 감기가 오려고 하나 봐.
B 냉방병에 걸리지 않도록 조심해.

DAY 072

어느 바쁜 날

🎧 Day 072

Things don't always go your way.

만사가 늘 원하는 대로 되진 않아.

MP3 강의 듣기

A Why do you keep **ignoring my text messages**?

B I was at the wheel*. I **had a tight schedule**.

A You're **bending over backwards** for your project.

B **Things don't always go your way**.

A Why don't we go get some sushi? My treat*.

B Perfect*. I know just the place*. You'll love it.

A 왜 내 문자에 답장 안 해?
B 운전 중이였어. 일정이 빠듯했어.
A 프로젝트 때문에 고생이 많구나.
B 만사가 늘 원하는 대로 되나.
A 초밥 먹으러 갈래? 내가 살게.
B 좋지. 딱 좋은 곳을 알아. 맘에 들 거야.

기타표현체크

- be at the wheel   운전 중이다
- perfect   좋아
- My treat   내가 낼게
- just the place   딱 좋은 곳

❶ ignore one's (text) message(s) 메시지를 무시하다

A Why have you been ignoring my messages all day?

B Don't be angry. My smartphone broke down.

A 왜 종일 내 문자에 답장을 안 하니?

B 화내지 마. 내 스마트폰이 고장 났어.

❷ have a tight schedule 일정이 빠듯하다

A We're going to a movie after work. Can you join us?

B I have a tight schedule today. Maybe next time.

A 퇴근 후 영화 보러 갈 건데. 같이 갈래?

B 오늘은 일정이 빠듯해. 다음에 같이 가자.

❸ bend over backwards (for+명사 / to+동사원형)
특별한 노력을 하다

A What is the most important thing in investing?

B You have to bend over backwards to raise seed capital.

A 투자하는 데 가장 중요한 게 뭐야?

B 무슨 수를 써서라도 종잣돈을 모아야지.

❹ Things don't always go your way
다 뜻대로 되진 않는다

A My plan fell through. All my efforts came to nothing.

B Think positive. Things don't always go your way.

A 내 계획이 무산됐어. 모든 노력이 허사가 됐어.

B 긍정적으로 생각해. 만사가 늘 뜻대로 되진 않아.

DAY 073

장거리 연애

🎧 Day 073

MP3 강의 듣기

Let's catch up over lunch.

점심 먹으며 얘기 좀 하자.

A I **got a cold sore in my mouth.** It hurts.

B You're still **having a long-distance relationship?**

A Yes, it's tough*. Let's **catch up over** lunch.

B Let's go grab* something you like.

A How about the Kimchi stew place* across the street*?

B **Are you okay with** spicy food? Let's go.

A 입안이 헐었어. 아파.

B 아직도 장거리 연애 중이니?

A 응, 힘드네. 점심 먹으며 얘기 하자.

B 너 좋아하는 거 먹으러 가자.

A 길 건너에 김치찌개 집 어때?

B 매운 음식 괜찮아? 가자.

기타표현체크

- tough 힘든
- kimchi stew place 김치찌개 집
- go grab sth ~을 먹으러 가다
- across the street 길 건너에

188

① get a cold sore in[on] one's mouth[lip]

입병이 나다

A I got a cold sore on my lower lip. What can I do?

B Apply this ointment to the wound. It'll work.

A 아랫입술에 입병이 났어요. 어떻게 해야 하죠?
B 이 연고를 상처에 바르세요. 효과 있을 겁니다.

② have a long-distance relationship

장거리 연애를 하다

A We're finally getting married. It doesn't feel real.

B Yeah. We've had a long-distance relationship.

A 마침내 우리가 결혼하는구나. 실감이 안 나.
B 그래. 그동안 장거리 연애를 했지.

③ catch up over + 음식[음료] ~을 먹으며 밀린 얘기를 하다

A Let's catch up over some drinks until late at night.

B Why don't we go to a place in my neighborhood?

A 밤늦게까지 술 마시며 얘기 좀 하자.
B 우리 동네 근처로 가는 건 어때?

④ Are you okay with sth? ~인데 괜찮겠어?

A Are you okay with ordering fried chicken?

B I'm sorry, but I want to have some pizza.

A 프라이드치킨 주문하려는데 어때?
B 미안한데 난 피자가 먹고 싶어.

DAY 074

That brings me back.

옛날 생각난다.

Day 074

MP3 강의 듣기

A I **got an invitation to** my college reunion.

B **That brings me back**. We had a ball* back then*.

A I'm a little depressed. **It** just **makes** me **feel** old.

B **Don't take it seriously.** Look how* well you're doing.

A I wonder how much they've changed.

B Have fun catching up with* everybody.

A 대학교 동창회 초대장을 받았어.
B 옛날 생각난다. 그땐 재미있었지.
A 좀 우울한데. 나이가 든 것 같아서.
B 심각하게 받아들이지 마. 잘 살고 있잖아.
A 친구들이 얼마나 변했는지 궁금해.
B 밀린 얘기하며 좋은 시간 보내.

기타표현체크

- have a ball   즐거운 시간을 보내다
- Look how 형/부 주어+동사   얼마나 ~하는지 봐라
- back then   그 시절엔
- catch up with sb   ~와 밀린 얘기를 하다

Mini Dialogues

❶ get an invitation to + 동사원형/명사 초대를 받다

A I got an invitation to visit my friend in Jeonju.

B You should check out the Hanok village. It'll be fun.

A 전주에 사는 친구한테 방문 요청을 받았어.

B 한옥마을에 꼭 가 봐. 재미있을 거야.

❷ That brings me back 옛날 생각난다

A Look at this picture! My son was really cute.

B That brings me back. I really miss that time.

A 이 사진 좀 봐! 우리 아들 정말 귀여웠어.

B 옛날 생각난다. 그때가 정말 그립다.

❸ It makes sb feel + 형용사 ~라는 느낌이 들다

A Mom, I got a prize in an English speech contest.

B I'm happy to hear that. It makes me feel proud.

A 엄마, 저 영어 말하기 대회에서 상 받았어요.

B 반가운 소식이네. 정말 뿌듯하구나.

❹ Don't take it seriously 심각하게 받아들이지 마

A I think she's really mad at me for being late.

B Don't take it too seriously. She will be okay.

A 내가 늦어서 그녀가 화가 많이 난 것 같아.

B 너무 심각하게 받아들이지 마. 괜찮을 거야.

191

DAY 075

You should put yourself in her place.

MP3 강의 듣기

그녀 입장에서 생각해 봐.

A Where are you off to* in such a hurry*?

B I'm going out for an annual family gathering*.

A Your family members have a strong bond* with each other.

B My mom always **nags** me **about** not getting married.

A You should **put yourself in her place.**

B I've **put a lot of effort** into that, but I'm **getting nowhere** with it.

A 그렇게 급히 어디 가는 거야?
B 연례 가족 모임에 가는 중이야.
A 가족끼리 서로 유대 관계가 좋구나.
B 엄마는 결혼 안 한다고 잔소리가 많으셔.
A 네가 엄마 입장이 되어 봐.
B 노력은 많이 했는데 성과가 없어.

기타표현체크

* Where are you off to? 어디 가는 길이야?   * in a hurry 급하게
* annual family gathering 연례 가족 모임   * have a strong bond (with) ~와 유대 관계가 좋다

❶ nag sb about sth(-ing) ~에 대해 잔소리하다

A My girlfriend always nags me about my weight.

B That's because she wants you to stay healthy.

A 여자 친구가 내 체중 때문에 늘 잔소리를 해.

B 네가 건강해지길 바라기 때문에 그러는 거야.

❷ put oneself in one's place[shoes]
입장 바꿔 생각하다

A I can't believe what she said to me yesterday.

B Nothing serious. Try to put yourself in her shoes.

A 어제 그녀가 나에게 한 말을 믿을 수가 없어.

B 별거 아니야. 그녀 입장에서 생각해 봐.

❸ put a lot of effort (into sth) ~에 노력을 많이 하다

A You're putting a lot of effort into editing your videos.

B That's what people say. Shooting is the tip of the iceberg.

A 비디오 편집에 엄청나게 노력을 많이 들이는구나.

B 다들 그렇게 말해. 촬영은 빙산의 일각일 뿐이야.

❹ get nowhere (with sb/sth) ~에 진전(성과)이 없다

A The trade war between US and China is raising concerns.

B Despite negotiations, they seem to be getting nowhere.

A 미 · 중 무역전쟁으로 우려가 제기되고 있어.

B 양국 간 협상에도 불구하고 진전은 없는 것 같아.

다음 주어진 우리말을 영어로 말해 보세요.

01 오늘 일진이 사납겠군.

----

02 운전 중이였어.

----

03 일정이 빠듯했어.

----

04 입안이 헐었어.

----

05 매운 음식 괜찮아?

----

06 옛날 생각난다.

----

07 심각하게 받아들이지 마.

----

08 어디 가는 길이야?

●정답 01. I'm having a bad hair day. 02. I was at the wheel. 03. I had a tight schedule. 04. I got a cold sore in my mouth. 05. Are you okay with spicy food? 06. That brings me back. 07. Don't take it seriously. 08. Where are you off to?

DAY
076~080

MP3와 저자 강의를 들어 보세요.

초보탈출!

DAY 076

It must've cost you a fortune.

MP3 강의 듣기

돈 많이 들었겠다.

A I got an electric car. It's called Model Y.

B It's cool. **It must've cost** you **a fortune**.

A EVs* will **become the norm** in the near future*.

B Many countries will ban* the sale of new fossil-fuel cars* from 2030.

A Tesla is **paving the way for** an era of EVs.

B They have **built a loyal fan base** globally.

A 전기 차 샀어. 모델 Y라고 해.
B 멋지다. 돈 많이 들었겠는데.
A 머지않아 전기 차가 대세가 될 거잖아.
B 많은 나라가 2030년부터 신규 내연 기관 차량 판매를 금지한대.
A 테슬라가 전기 차 시대를 앞장서고 있어.
B 세계적으로 충성 팬층을 구축했지.

기타표현체크

- EVs(Electric Vehicles) 전기 자동차
- ban sth ~을 금지하다
- in the near future 머지않아
- fossil-fuel cars 내연 기관 차량

❶ cost (sb) a fortune 큰돈이 들다.

A I bought a four-bedroom house for my family.
B It must've cost you a fortune. When are you moving?

A 가족을 위해 침실 4개짜리 집을 샀어.
B 돈 많이 들었겠다. 언제 이사할 거야?

---

❷ become the norm 대세가 되다

A Influencer marketing is becoming the norm lately.
B We can't sell anything without using Youtube channel.

A 요즘 유명인 마케팅이 점점 대세가 되고 있어.
B 유튜브 채널을 활용하지 않고 판매를 할 수가 없지.

---

❸ pave the way for sb/sth ~를 위해 앞장서다, 길을 닦다

A It's important for parents to read books for their kids.
B They can pave the way for their kids to read.

A 부모가 독서하는 것은 아이들에게 중요합니다.
B 자녀가 독서를 할 수 있게 앞장서는 거죠.

---

❹ build a (loyal) fan base (충성스러운) 팬층을 구축하다

A BTS top the list on the billboard chart once again.
B Their amazing songs helped to build a fan base.

A BTS가 다시 한 번 빌보드 차트 1위를 차지했어.
B 멋진 노래가 팬층을 구축하는 데 도움이 됐지.

엄마의 장난

Day 077

DAY 077

It's written on your face.

얼굴에 쓰여 있어요.

MP3 강의 듣기

A Mom! Did you **put** my phone **away**?

B Keep looking. It must be somewhere.

A Please don't tell me* you've hidden it.

B You **catch on quick.** How did you **pick up on** that?

A I can tell* right away. It's written on your face*.

B **Your battery was dead.** So, I'm charging* it.

A 엄마! 제 전화기 치우셨어요?
B 잘 찾아봐. 어딘가 있겠지.
A 설마 숨겨 두신 건 아니죠?
B 눈치 빠르네. 어떻게 알아차렸니?
A 보면 알죠. 얼굴에 다 쓰여 있어요.
B 배터리가 없던데. 충전하고 있어.

기타표현체크

• Don't tell me **주어+동사**   설마 ~하는 건 아니겠지?
• be written on one's face   얼굴에 쓰여 있다

• tell   알아차리다
• charge sth   ~을 충전하다

198

❶ put sth away ~을 치우다

A I'll vacuum the floor. Can you put your stuff away?

B Sure. I'll do that after I finish what I'm doing.

A 바닥 청소를 하려는데. 네 물건 좀 치워 줄래?

B 알겠어요. 지금 하던 거 끝내고 할게요.

❷ catch on quick 눈치가(이해가) 빠르다

A You did the dishes. You want something from me?

B You catch on quick. Can I get some allowance?

A 설거지를 했네. 나한테 바라는 거 있니?

B 눈치 빠르시네요. 용돈 좀 주실래요?

❸ pick up on sth 간파하다, 알아차리다

A She dumped me. I've never felt this way before.

B Didn't you pick up on it? She doesn't love you.

A 그녀한테 차였어. 이런 느낌 처음이야.

B 눈치 못 챘어? 그녀는 널 사랑하지 않아.

❹ one's battery is[go] dead 배터리가 떨어지다

A My battery went dead. Do you have a backup battery?

B Yes. I brought it just in case. Better safe than sorry.

A 배터리가 떨어졌어. 보조 배터리 있니?

B 응. 만약을 위해 가져왔지. 유비무환이잖아.

DAY 078

We're always short-handed.

늘 일손이 부족해.

A What are you up to* tonight?

B Nothing much*. Maybe I'll be **working like a dog**.

A All work and no play makes Jack a dull boy.*

B I know. But we're always short-handed*.

A Besides, we don't **get paid extra for overtime**.

B **It burns me up**. I'm **having a mental breakdown**.

A 오늘 저녁에 무슨 계획 있어?
B 특별한 건 없어. 열심히 일하고 있겠지.
A 너무 일만 하는 건 너한테 좋지 않아.
B 알아. 근데 늘 일손이 부족하잖아.
A 게다가, 야근 수당도 못 받잖아.
B 열 받네. 너무 충격적이야.

기타표현체크

- What are you up to? 뭐하고 지내?/뭐할 거야?
- Nothing much 별일 없다
- All work and no play makes Jack a dull boy. 일만 하고 놀지 않으면 바보가 된다 (속담)
- short-handed 일손이 부족한

① work like a dog 열심히 일하다

A I took out a loan to buy a house. I should tighten my belt.

B So did I. I'm working like a dog to pay off the debt.

A 집 사려고 대출받았어. 허리띠 졸라매야 해.

B 나도 그랬어. 빚 갚으려고 열심히 일하고 있지.

② get paid extra for overtime 초과 근무 수당을 받다

A I got burned out since I worked overtime last night.

B It's a good thing you can get paid extra for overtime.

A 어젯밤에 야근하느라 완전히 지쳤어.

B 초과 근무 수당이라도 받아서 다행이야.

③ It burns me up (to+동사원형) ~하다니 열 받네

A She has been talking about you behind your back.

B It burns me up to hear that. I was nice to her.

A 그녀가 뒤에서 네 험담을 하고 다녔데.

B 듣고 보니 열 받네. 내가 잘해 줬는데.

④ have a mental breakdown (정신적으로) 큰 충격을 받다

A My stocks plunged more than 10% yesterday.

B Are you okay? You're having a mental breakdown.

A 어제 내 주식이 10% 넘게 폭락했어.

B 괜찮아? 충격이 크겠구나.

DAY 079

I pulled a muscle in my neck.

목을 삐끗했어.

MP3 강의 듣기

A I think I **pulled a muscle in** my neck.

B I told you to stretch as often as possible*.

A I'm going to take a Pilates class* like you.

B Good thinking*, but you shouldn't **rush into** it.

A **I can't be bothered** to do anything because I **feel under the weather.**

B Try to keep exercising and stay in shape*.

A 나 목을 삐끗한 것 같아.
B 스트레칭을 가능한 한 자주 하라고 했잖아.
A 너처럼 필라테스 강습을 받아야겠다.
B 잘 생각했어. 근데 서두르지는 마.
A 몸이 안 좋으니까 만사가 다 귀찮아.
B 꾸준히 운동해서 건강을 유지해.

기타표현체크

• as often as possible   최대한 자주
• Good thinking   잘 생각했어
• take a Pilates class   필라테스 강습을 받다
• stay in shape   건강(몸매)을 유지하다

❶ pull a muscle in (신체 부위) ~ 근육을 삐끗하다

A I pulled a muscle in my back trying to pick up something.

B You should see a doctor before it gets worse.

A 물건을 들다가 허리를 삐끗했어.
B 더 악화되기 전에 병원에 가 봐.

❷ rush into sth 성급하게 행동하다, 서두르다

A Are you still going out with her? Why not get married?

B I don't want to rush into marriage. I'll take it slow.

A 그녀와 아직 사귀니? 왜 결혼을 안 해?
B 서둘러 하고 싶진 않아. 천천히 할 거야.

❸ I can't be bothered (to 동사원형/with 명사)
~하기 귀찮다

A Mom, I'm starving. What's up for tonight?

B I can't be bothered with cooking. Let's eat out.

A 엄마, 배가 많이 고파요. 저녁에 뭐 먹어요?
B 요리하기 귀찮은데. 우리 나가서 먹자.

❹ feel under the weather 몸이 안 좋다

A Why did you miss the workshop last week?

B I was feeling under the weather at the time.

A 지난주 워크숍에 왜 안 왔어?
B 그때는 몸이 좀 안 좋았어.

DAY 080

They walked down the aisle.

MP3 강의 듣기

결혼식을 했어.

A I was told that* Tom **got a divorce**.

B No kidding! They have been separated*.

A They **walked down the aisle** just months ago.

B I can't believe that. You live and learn*.

A It really **gets** me **down.** I don't know how I can comfort* him.

B Me neither. I **fell out of touch with** him recently.

A 톰이 이혼했다고 들었어.

B 설마! 걔네들 별거 중이었잖아.

A 결혼한 지 몇 달 안 됐는데.

B 믿을 수가 없어. 별일이 다 있네.

A 우울해지네. 어떻게 위로해야 할지 모르겠어.

B 나도 그래. 최근에 걔랑 연락이 끊겼어.

기타표현체크

• I was told that ~ ~라고 듣다
• live and learn 별일이 다 있다
• be separated 별거하다
• comfort sb ~를 위로하다

❶ get a divorce 이혼하다

A Did you hear that they got a divorce?

B Yes. They have been separated for 5 years.

A 그들이 이혼했다는 소식 들었어?

B 그래. 두 사람 서로 5년째 별거 중이었어.

❷ walk down the aisle 결혼하다

A Here's a wedding invitation. Please come to celebrate.

B Finally, you two are walking down the aisle.

A 여기 청첩장입니다. 와서 축하해 주세요.

B 드디어 너희 둘이 결혼하는구나.

❸ get sb down ~을 우울하게 하다

A Nothing works out for me. Why am I like this?

B Don't let it get you down. You can pull it off.

A 되는 일이 하나도 없어. 난 왜 이럴까?

B 의기소침하지 마. 넌 해낼 거야.

❹ fall out of touch with sb ~와 연락이 끊기다

A Do you keep in touch with Tom? You guys were tight.

B I've fallen out of touch with him since graduation.

A 톰하고 연락하니? 너희들 친했잖아.

B 졸업한 이후로 연락이 끊겼어.

다음 주어진 우리말을 영어로 말해 보세요.

01 돈 많이 들었겠다.

---

02 눈치 빠르네.

---

03 배터리가 없던데.

---

04 오늘 저녁에 무슨 계획 있어?

---

05 늘 일손이 부족하잖아.

---

06 목을 삐끗했어.

---

07 톰이 이혼했어.

---

08 별일이 다 있네.

●정답 01. It must've cost you a fortune.   02. You catch on quick.   03. Your battery was dead.
04. What are you up to tonight?   05. We're always short-handed.   06. I pulled a muscle in my neck.
07. Tom got a divorce.   08. You live and learn.

DAY
081~085

MP3와 저자 강의를 들어 보세요.

DAY 081

MP3 강의 듣기

Keep up the good work.

계속 열심히 해.

A Why are you biting your nails*?

B Well, I **quit** smoking **cold turkey** a few days ago.

A You're having withdrawal symptoms*. **Keep up the good work.**

B You're in no place to* talk to me like that.

A You got me*. I'll **give up** smoking soon.

B I'm going to **give it a try**. I'll try anything.

A 왜 손톱을 물어뜯는 거니?
B 며칠 전에 갑자기 담배를 끊었거든.
A 금단 현상이네. 계속 열심히 해.
B 그렇게 말할 처지는 아니잖아.
A 할 말이 없네. 곧 담배를 끊을 거야.
B 한번 해 볼 거야. 뭐든 해야지.

기타표현체크

- bite one's nails 손톱을 물어뜯다
- be in no place to+동사원형 ~할 입장이 아니다
- withdrawal symptoms 금단 현상
- You got me 할 말이 없네

❶ quit (sth) cold turkey (나쁜 습관을) 갑자기 끊다

A My son plays online games so much. What should I do?
B It's hard to quit cold turkey. He needs other activities.

A 아들이 온라인 게임을 너무 많이 해. 내가 어떻게 해야 할까?
B 갑자기 그만두기는 힘들어. 다른 활동이 필요해.

❷ keep up the good work 계속 열심히 해

A Your grades are good. Keep up the good work.
B Thank you. It's all thanks to you, teacher.

A 성적이 좋구나. 계속 열심히 해.
B 감사합니다. 모두 선생님 덕분입니다.

❸ give up + (동)명사 ~를 끊다, 포기하다

A I'm not cut out for this job. I'm going to quit.
B Don't give up. You'll get the hang of it soon.

A 이 일은 내 적성에 안 맞아. 그만둘 거야.
B 포기하지 마. 곧 요령을 터득하게 될 거야.

❹ give it a try 한번 해 보다

A Just go by the book. I don't want to take any chances.
B Why don't you give it a try? You have nothing to lose.

A 원칙대로 해. 모험하고 싶지 않아.
B 한번 해 봐. 손해 볼 건 없어.

I didn't get a wink of sleep.

MP3 강의 듣기

한숨도 못 잤어.

A I think your eyes are swollen*.

B I didn't get a wink of sleep last night.

A Take a quick nap during lunch break*.

B Luckily, my boss is on a business trip today.

A But we need to attend a video conference later.

B I'm not myself* today. It's going to be a long day*.

A 너 눈이 부은 것 같아.
B 어젯밤에 한숨도 못 잤어.
A 점심 때 잠깐 눈 좀 붙여.
B 다행히 오늘 부장님이 출장 가셨어.
A 근데 우리 이따가 화상 회의에 참석해야 해.
B 오늘 제정신이 아니야. 긴 하루가 되겠군.

기타표현체크

· swollen 부은
· be not oneself 제정신이 아니다

· during lunch break 점심 시간에
· long day 긴 하루, 힘든 하루

❶ don't[can't] get a wink of sleep 한숨도 못 자다

A I couldn't get a wink of sleep for a few days.

B Again? Since when did the problem begin?

A 며칠 동안 잠을 한숨도 못 잤어.

B 또? 언제부터 불면증이 생겼어?

❷ take a quick nap (잠시) 낮잠을 자다

A If you feel sleepy, go and get some sleep.

B I'll take a quick nap. Wake me up in 20 minutes.

A 졸리면 가서 눈 좀 붙여.

B 잠깐 잘게. 20분 후에 깨워 줘.

❸ be[go] on a business trip 출장 중이다[가다]

A I'm going on a business trip to China next week.

B Really? We were supposed to meet that night.

A 다음 주에 중국으로 출장을 떠날 거야.

B 정말? 그날 저녁에 만나기로 했잖아.

❹ attend a video conference 화상 회의에 참석하다

A I attended a video conference during my business trip.

B Times have changed a lot thanks to IT technology.

A 출장 중에 화상 회의에 참석했어.

B IT기술 덕에 세상이 정말 많이 변했어.

DAY 083

건강이 최고야

Day 083

MP3 강의 듣기

I was passed over for a promotion.

나 승진에서 탈락했어.

A I **was passed over** for a promotion.

B That's a shame*. Let's have pork belly with soju*.

A Thanks, but my stomach **is bothering me**.

B I guess you **worry too much about** it.

A No. Actually, I'm just tired. That's all.

B I get the picture*. **Take care of yourself.**

A 나 승진에서 탈락했어.
B 안타깝다. 삼겹살에 소주 한잔 하자.
A 고맙긴 한데, 속이 좀 안 좋아서.
B 신경을 너무 많이 써서 그런가 봐.
A 아니. 조금 피곤해서. 그것 뿐이야.
B 알았어. 몸 관리 잘해.

기타표현체크

- That's a shame   안타깝다, 아쉽다
- get the picture   (상황을) 이해하다
- pork belly with soju   삼겹살과 소주

Mini Dialogues

1 **be passed over (for sth)** ~에서 제외되다

A It's ridiculous. I was next in line for a promotion.
B Are you serious? Why did they pass you over?

A 말도 안 돼. 난 이번 승진 대상이었는데.
B 정말이야? 왜 네가 제외된 거지?

2 **sth is bothering sb** ~ 때문에 불편하다

A The rising cost of living bothers me a lot.
B Right. It's hard to live on this salary.

A 요즘 치솟는 생활비 때문에 걱정이야.
B 맞아. 이 월급으로 생계를 유지하기 힘들어.

3 **worry too much about sth** ~를 너무 신경 쓰다

A You don't seem to have any interest in fashion.
B I don't worry too much about what people think.

A 넌 패션에 대해 별로 관심이 없는 것 같아.
B 사람들이 어떻게 생각하는지 크게 신경 쓰지 않아.

4 **take care of yourself** 몸 관리 잘해

A I hope you'll get better soon. Take care of yourself.
B Thanks. I'll see you after I check out of the hospital.

A 곧 쾌차하기 바라고 몸조리 잘해.
B 고마워. 퇴원하고 나서 보자.

213

🎧 Day 084

MP3 강의 듣기

DAY 084

I'll treat you to dinner tonight.

오늘 저녁에 식사 대접할게요.

A Hi, dad. Is mom in*? It's mom's birthday.

B **It's so sweet of you to** remember. I'll **put her on.**
(Mother picks up the phone*.)

C Hey, honey! It's been a long time*. What's up?

A Happy birthday, mom. I'll **treat you to** dinner tonight.
I'm going to drop by* after I **get off work.**

C Thanks. We can decide where to go later.

A 아빠, 엄마 계세요? 엄마 생신이잖아요.
B 기억해 줘서 고맙구나. 엄마 바꿔 줄게. (엄마가 전화를 받는다.)
C 안녕, 얘야. 오랜만이구나. 어쩐 일이야?
A 생신 축하드려요, 엄마. 저녁에 식사 대접할게요. 퇴근하고 들를게요.
C 고마워. 어디로 갈지는 만나서 결정하자.

기타표현체크

- Is sb in? ~ 있어요?
- It's been a long time 오랜만이다
- pick up the phone 전화를 받다
- drop by 들르다

❶ It's sweet of sb to + 동사원형 ~해 줘서 고마워

A I'm sorry that I didn't call sooner. It's my fault.
B That's sweet of you to say so. You're a peach.

A 미리 전화 못 해서 미안해요. 제 잘못이에요.
B 그렇게 말해 줘서 고마워요. 친절하시네요.

❷ put sb on (the phone) ~에게 전화를 바꿔 주다

A Hello, Gina. This is Frank, Can I speak to George?
B Sure. Hold on please. I'll put him on the phone?

A 안녕, 지나. 프랭크예요. 조지와 통화할 수 있나요?
B 물론이죠. 잠시만 기다리세요. 연결해 드릴게요.

❸ treat sb to + 음식/식사 ~를 대접하다

A Thank you for your time. I'll be in touch with you.
B I enjoyed the meal. I'll treat you to something soon.

A 시간 내 주셔서 감사합니다. 연락 드리겠습니다.
B 잘 먹었어요. 조만간 제가 대접할게요.

❹ get off work 퇴근하다

A Honey, can you get off work early tomorrow?
B I'm talking with a client. I'll call you back later.

A 자기야, 내일 좀 일찍 퇴근할 수 있어?
B 고객과 이야기 중이야. 나중에 전화할게.

DAY 085

어깨 통증

Day 085

MP3 강의 듣기

My shoulder hurts like hell.

어깨가 엄청 아파.

A You don't seem to be feeling well.

B My right shoulder **hurts like hell.**

I'm going to take sick leave* for a few days.

A You've **overworked yourself.** Take it easy*.

B **Talk is cheap.** I almost missed a deadline*.

A Lighten up. **That's the way** it **goes.**

B Thanks. You're the best.

A 몸이 안 좋아 보이는데.
B 우측 어깨가 너무 아파. 며칠 병가 내려고.
A 무리했구나. 쉬엄쉬엄해.
B 말은 쉽지. 마감일도 겨우 지켰어.
A 기운 내. 세상사가 다 그렇지.
B 고마워. 너밖에 없구나.

기타표현체크

- take sick leave   병가를 내다
- miss a deadline   마감일을 놓치다
- take it easy   쉬엄쉬엄하다
- Lighten up   기운 내

216

① sth hurts like hell ~가 너무 아프다

A Good afternoon. What seems to be the trouble?
B When I raise my hand, it hurts like hell right here.

A 안녕하세요. 어디가 불편하세요?
B 어깨를 올리면 여기가 엄청 아파요.

② overwork oneself 과로하다, 무리하다

A You look better than ever. What's your secret?
B I don't overwork myself. I get enough sleep every night.

A 어느 때보다 좋아 보이는데. 비결이 뭐야?
B 무리하지 않아. 매일 충분히 자고.

③ Talk is cheap 말이야 쉽지

A The lawyers asked for a delay in the trial date.
B Talk is cheap. It's going to be held on schedule.

A 변호인들이 재판 날짜 연기를 신청했어.
B 말이야 쉽지. 예정대로 열릴 거야.

④ That's the way sth goes ~이란 그런 거야

A I'm crazy about her. I can't stop thinking about her.
B That's the way love goes. It makes you blind.

A 그녀에게 빠졌어. 그녀에 대한 생각을 멈출 수가 없어.
B 사랑이란 그런 거야. 눈을 멀게 하지.

다음 주어진 우리말을 영어로 말해 보세요.

01 갑자기 담배를 끊었어.

----

02 뭐든 해야지.

----

03 너 눈이 부었어.

----

04 부장님이 출장 가셨어.

----

05 나 승진에서 탈락했어.

----

06 속이 좀 안 좋아

----

07 기억해 줘서 고맙구나.

----

08 말은 쉽지.

●정답 01. I quit smoking cold turkey 02. I'll try anything. 03. Your eyes are swollen. 04. My boss is on a business trip today. 05. I was passed over for a promotion. 06. My stomach is bothering me. 07. It's so sweet of you to remember. 08. Talk is cheap.

DAY
086~090

MP3와 저자 강의를 들어 보세요.

DAY 086

고속도로 휴게소

🎧 Day 086

MP3 강의 듣기

I'm always behind you.

난 늘 네 편이야.

A Have you packed everything? Hop in*!

B Dad, will you drop by the rest area?

A I can **see right through** you. You want to have snacks*.

B Don't get me wrong*. I don't **take the easy way out.**

A I'm just joking. I'm always **behind** you.

B You **made my day.** Let's get a move on*.

A 물건 다 챙겼지? 어서 타.
B 아빠, 휴게소 들르실 거예요?
A 네 속셈 알아. 군것질하고 싶구나.
B 오해하지 마세요. 잔머리 쓰는 거 아니에요.
A 농담이야. 아빠는 늘 네 편이야.
B 아빠 덕분에 행복해요. 어서 가요.

기타표현체크

- hop in (the car) (차에) 타다
- Don't get me wrong 오해하지 마세요
- have snacks 군것질하다
- get a move on 서두르다

220

Mini Dialogues

1. see right through sb ~를 꿰뚫어 보다

A He goes to the restroom when it's time to pay.
B I can see right through him. He's so cheap.

A 그는 계산할 때 화장실에 가.
B 속셈이 뻔하지. 걔 엄청 짠돌이야.

2. take the easy way out 쉬운 길을 택하다, 잔머리 쓰다

A I don't want to go to college. I want to make money.
B Don't take the easy way out. I bet you'll be sorry.

A 대학에 가고 싶지 않아요. 돈을 벌게요.
B 쉬운 길을 선택하지 마. 후회하게 될 거야.

3. be behind sb ~를 지지하다, ~의 배후에 있다

A It's like I'm always stuck in second gear.
B I'm sure you can manage it. We are behind you.

A 난 항상 일이 제대로 되지 않는 것 같아.
B 어떻게든 해낼 꺼야. 우리가 있잖아

4. make one's day ~를 기쁘게 하다

A Congrats! Your son's baseball team made it to the finals.
B Thank you so much. That news really made my day.

A 축하해! 네 아들 야구팀이 결승에 진출했다면서.
B 정말 고마워. 그 소식 덕분에 너무 기뻤어.

DAY 087

육아의 달인

Day 087
MP3 강의 듣기

You have a way with kids.

아이들을 잘 다루는구나.

A You **have a way with** kids. How can you do that?

B **My experience tells me that** scolding* them is not working*.

A I need to **brush up** on my parenting skills*.

B You're humble*. You know better than I.

A How about your husband? Is he doing okay?

B He's fine. He **doesn't touch alcohol** nowadays.

A 아이들을 잘 다루네. 어떻게 하는 거야?
B 내 경험에 의하면 잔소리는 효과가 없어.
A 나도 양육 기술을 좀 연마해야겠다.
B 겸손하긴. 네가 나보다 더 잘 알잖아.
A 네 남편은 어때? 잘 지내지?
B 잘 지내. 요즘 술을 입에도 안 대.

기타표현체크

• scold 꾸짖다, 야단치다
• parenting skill 양육 기술
• work 효과가 있다
• humble 겸손한

❶ have a way with sth/sb ~을 잘 다루다

A How is your new employee? Is he adapting well?
B He's doing great. He has a way with customers.

A 신입 사원 어때요? 잘 적응하고 있나요?
B 잘하고 있어요. 고객 응대를 정말 잘 해요.

❷ My experience tells me that 주어+동사
내 경험에 따르면 ~이다

A Why are you doing that? It doesn't seem to be related.
B My experience tells me that this will be helpful.

A 왜 그걸 하는 거야? 관련이 없는 것 같은데.
B 내 경험에 따르면 이게 도움이 될 거야.

❸ brush up (on) sth ~을 연마하다; 복습하다

A You finally got into NYU thanks to your English skills.
B I need to brush up on my English before I go to college.

A 영어 실력 덕분에 마침내 뉴욕 대학에 입학했구나.
B 학교 가기 전에 영어 좀 연습해야겠어.

❹ don't touch alcohol 술을 전혀 안 마시다

A He got stopped for a DUI and had to pay a penalty.
B That's why he hasn't touched alcohol for some time.

A 그는 음주 운전으로 걸려서 벌금을 냈어.
B 그래서 한동안 술을 입에 안 댔구나.

* DUI(Driving Under Influence) 음주 운전

I'm biting the bullet.

이를 악물고 버티고 있어.

A What's new with you* these days?

B I'm **biting the bullet.** I've been stuck in* the office.

A I've been **working far away from home** for 5 years.

B Oh, man! I **know what it's like to** be alone.

A My wife wants me* to **take paternity leave.**

B You can take advantage of* it when you need it.

A 요즘 별일 없어?
B 죽겠어. 사무실에서 일만 해.
A 가족과 떨어져 일한 지 5년째야.
B 저런! 혼자 지내는 게 어떤 건지 알아.
A 아내는 내가 육아 휴직하기를 원해.
B 필요할 때 활용해야지.

기타표현체크

• What's new with you? 별일 없어?
• want sb to+동사원형 ~가 ~하기를 원하다
• be stuck in+(장소) 명사 ~에 갇혀 있다
• take advantage of sth ~을 이용하다

Mini Dialogues

❶ bite the bullet 이를 악물고 견디다

A I hate it when I have to clean up after somebody.

B I know it's hard, but you have to bite the bullet.

A 다른 사람 뒤처리하는 거 정말 싫어.
B 힘든 줄 알지만, 꾹 참고 견뎌야 해.

---

❷ work far away from home 가족과 떨어져서 일하다

A You'll miss your family working far away from home.

B I feel bad that I can't spend more time with my kids.

A 집 떠나 멀리서 일하니 가족이 보고 싶겠다.
B 아이들과 시간을 더 못 보내는 게 미안하지.

---

❸ know what it's like to + 동사원형 ~가 어떤 건지 알다

A Making lots of money is not the only way to success.

B I don't know what it's like to be successful in life.

A 돈을 많이 버는 게 성공하는 유일한 길은 아니야.
B 인생에서 성공하는 게 어떤 건지 모르겠어.

---

❹ take paternity(maternity) leave
육아 휴직을 내다

A It's common for fathers to take paternity leave nowadays.

B They can provide a different kind of emotional attachment.

A 요즘 아빠들이 육아 휴직을 내는 게 흔해졌어.
B 또 다른 정서적 애착을 줄 수 있으니까.

Are you adding fuel to the fire?

불난 집에 부채질하니?

A I'm going crazy. I screwed up my math test.

B You can do better next time. I think I aced* it.

A Say what*? Are you adding fuel to the fire?

B Good grades don't always bring you success.

A Get over yourself!* You have an attitude problem.

B Don't blow your top. You need to curb your temper*.

A 미치겠네. 수학 시험을 망쳤어.
B 다음에 잘하면 되지. 난 잘 본 것 같아.
A 뭐라고? 불난 집에 부채질하는 거니?
B 공부 잘한다고 꼭 성공하는 건 아니잖아.
A 잘난 척 하지 마. 넌 태도가 문제야.
B 발끈하지 마. 성질 좀 죽여.

기타표현체크

- ace sth   ~을 잘 해내다
- Get over yourself!   잘난 척 하지 마!
- say what   (놀라서) 뭐라고?
- curb one's temper   화를 참다

226

① screw up sth ~을 망치다

A It's been raining for three days. It screwed up my weekend.

B This monsoon season seems longer than usual.

A 비가 3일째 내리고 있네. 주말을 망쳐 버렸어.

B 이번 장마는 여느 때보다 긴 것 같아.

② add fuel to the fire 상황을 악화시키다, 불난 집에 부채질하다

A I heard she is in trouble. How did it go with the police?

B Her lies added fuel to the fire. She had to quit her job.

A 그녀가 어려움에 처했다면서. 경찰하고 일은 어떻게 됐어?

B 거짓말로 인해 상황이 악화됐어. 일을 그만둬야 한대.

③ A doesn't always bring B

A라고 해서 항상 B 하는 것은 아니다

A I don't want to get by on a small income anymore.

B Neither do I, but riches do not always bring happiness.

A 더 이상 적은 수입으로 근근하게 살고 싶지 않아.

B 나도 그래. 하지만 부가 늘 행복을 가져오진 않아.

④ blow one's top 발끈하다, 버럭 화를 내다

A How could you stand it? If I were you, I'd blow my top.

B There was nothing I could do. I had to be patient.

A 어떻게 참았어? 나였으면 폭발했을 거야.

B 뭐 어쩌겠어. 내가 참을 수밖에.

227

We're behind schedule.

예정보다 늦어졌어요.

A Can you check if* I need to make any alterations*?

B Sorry, but I'll be **attending a meeting** now.

A I'm in a rush. We**'re behind schedule.**

B As I recall*, the deadline has been extended.

A Are you sure? I'll **check with** my boss.

B The sooner, the better*. We always finish **in the nick of time.**

A 수정할 사항이 있는지 확인해 줄래요?
B 미안한데 지금 회의에 참석해야 해요.
A 좀 급해요. 예정보다 늦어져서요.
B 제가 기억하기로는 마감일이 연장되었어요.
A 정말요? 부장님한테 확인해 볼게요.
B 빠를수록 좋죠. 늘 빠듯하게 끝내잖아요.

기타표현체크

• **check if 주어+동사** ~할 수 있는지 확인하다
• **as I recall** 제 기억으로는
• **make alterations (to) sth** ~를 수정하다
• **the sooner, the better** 빠를수록 좋다

❶ attend a meeting 회의에 참석하다

A Who is gonna attend the monthly meeting this time?

B My boss will be there in person. I'm his secretary.

A 이번에는 월례 회의에 누가 참석하실 건가요?

B 저희 사장님이 직접 가십니다. 제가 비서입니다.

❷ be behind[ahead of] schedule 일정보다 늦다[앞서다]

A When can I get your first draft? The deadline is coming up.

B Not to worry. I'm a few weeks ahead of schedule.

A 초고는 언제 받을 수 있나요? 마감일이 다가와요.

B 걱정 마세요. 예정보다 몇 주 앞서가고 있어요.

❸ check with sb ~와 상담(확인)하다

A I'm writing a paper. What is your annual sales goal?

B I can't answer it right now. I'll check with the manager.

A 보고서 작성 중입니다. 연간 매출 목표가 어떻게 되죠?

B 바로 답변 드릴 수 없네요. 담당자에게 확인해 볼게요.

❹ 동사 + in the nick of time 아슬아슬하게 ~ 하다

A Did you arrive safely? You left 10 minutes late.

B Fortunately I got to the terminal in the nick of time.

A 안전하게 도착했어? 너 10분 늦게 출발했잖아.

B 다행히 터미널에 아슬아슬하게 도착했어.

Review Quiz — Day 086-090

다음 주어진 우리말을 영어로 말해 보세요.

01 물건 다 챙겼지?

----

02 난 늘 네 편이야.

----

03 아이들을 잘 다루는구나.

----

04 네가 나보다 더 잘 알잖아.

----

05 요즘 별일 없어?

----

06 이를 악물고 버티고 있어.

----

07 다음에 잘하면 되지.

----

08 예정보다 늦어졌어요.

정답 01. Have you packed everything?   02. I'm always behind you.   03. You have a way with kids.
04. You know better than I.   05. What's new with you these days?   06. I'm biting the bullet.   07. You can do better next time.   08. We're behind schedule.

DAY
091~095

MP3와 저자 강의를 들어 보세요.

MP3 강의 듣기

I can't get enough of sushi.

초밥은 아무리 먹어도 안 질려.

A **What are your plans for** this Saturday?

B Maybe I'll catch up on* my reading at home.

A Didn't you say* you have a family gathering*?

B **It has been postponed until** next week for my brother.

A How about* having some sushi? I know a new place.

   You can **get a lot for your money**.

B Why not? I **can't get enough of** sushi.

A 이번 주 토요일에 뭐할 거야?
B 집에서 밀린 독서를 할 것 같아.
A 가족 모임이 있다고 하지 않았니?
B 남동생 때문에 다음 주로 연기됐어.
A 초밥 먹을래? 새로 생긴 곳을 아는데 가성비가 좋아.
B 좋지. 초밥은 아무리 먹어도 질리지 않아.

기타표현체크

· catch up on+(동)명사 밀린 일을 하다.   · Didn't you say (that) 주어+동사 ～라고 하지 않았어?
· have a family gathering 가족 모임을 하다 · How about+(동)명사 ～하는 건 어때?

 **Mini Dialogues**

❶ What are your plans for + (시간) 명사?

~에 계획이 있나요?

A What are your plans for the coming year?

B My new year's resolution is to learn how to swim.

A 내년에는 어떤 계획이 있어?

B 새해 다짐은 수영을 배우는 거야.

❷ be postponed until + 시간 명사　~로 연기되다

A The business trip has been postponed until next Tuesday.

B I won't be able to join you. I have a schedule conflict.

A 출장이 다음 주 화요일로 연기되었어.

B 난 같이 못 갈 거 같아. 다른 일정이 있어.

❸ get a lot for one's money　가성비가 좋다

A This line is taking forever. When can we get to eat?

B Just hang in there. You can get a lot for your money.

A 엄청 기다려야겠네. 언제 먹을 수 있는 거야?

B 조금만 참아. 가성비가 제법 괜찮거든.

❹ can't get enough of sth　아무리 ~해도 질리지 않다

A I've started watching *Kingdom* on Netflix.

B I love that drama. I can't get enough of it.

A 넷플릭스에서 〈킹덤〉을 보기 시작했어.

B 나도 그 드라마 좋아해. 아무리 봐도 질리지 않아.

How did you get by without the phone?

휴대폰 없이 어떻게 버텼어?

A I've been calling you* all day. I couldn't reach you*.

B Sorry. I think I left my cell phone at home.

A It must've been tough. How did you **get by without** it?

B It was good because I didn't have to **waste my time worrying about the small stuff.**

A Don't tell me* you did that on purpose*.

B Come on. **Don't be a drama queen.**

A 하루 종일 전화했어. 연락이 안 되던데.
B 미안. 휴대폰을 집에 두고 온 것 같아.
A 힘들었겠네. 휴대폰 없이 어떻게 버텼어?
B 사소한 일에 신경 안 써도 되니 좋던데.
A 설마 일부러 그런 건 아니겠지?
B 왜 이래? 오버 좀 하지 마.

기타표현체크

- have been calling sb   ~에게 계속 전화하다
- Don't tell me 주어+동사   설마 ~하는 건 아니겠지
- reach sb   ~에게 연락이 닿다
- on purpose   고의로

❶ get by without sb/sth ~없이 지내다

A You spend most of your time playing online games.

B I can't get by without them. I promise to study hard.

A 대부분의 시간을 온라인 게임하는 데 보내는구나.
B 게임 없으면 못 살아요. 공부 열심히 할게요.

❷ waste one's time -ing ~하느라 시간을 낭비하다

A I can't get over the fact that I got ripped off.

B Don't waste your time thinking about the past.

A 내가 바가지를 썼다는 사실이 안 믿겨져.
B 과거를 생각하느라 시간을 낭비하지 마.

❸ worry about the small stuff 작은 일에 신경을 쓰다

A You look healthy. How do you manage your stress?

B Most of all, I don't worry about the small stuff.

A 건강해 보인다. 너는 어떻게 스트레스를 관리해?
B 무엇보다 작은 일에 신경을 안 쓰는 거지.

❹ Don't be a drama queen 호들갑 떨지 마, 오버 하지 마

A Where have you been? It's time to leave.

B Take it easy. Don't be such a drama queen.

A 어디 갔었어? 출발할 시간이야.
B 진정해. 호들갑 좀 떨지 마.

I'm feeling much better.

MP3 강의 듣기

많이 좋아진 것 같아.

A How are you feeling this morning?

B I'm **feeling much better** than yesterday.
But I still **have a runny nose.**

A Did you **take medicine?** Drink as much water as possible*.

B Thanks. Today I'll go to see a doctor* again.

A You should get a shot*. It'll help you get through* it.

B Okay. I'll try to **get enough rest** tonight.

A 오늘 아침 컨디션이 어때?
B 어제보다 훨씬 좋아졌어. 근데 아직 콧물이 나.
A 약은 먹었지? 가능한 한 물을 많이 마셔.
B 고마워. 오늘 다시 병원에 가봐야겠어.
A 주사 좀 맞아. 낫는 데 도움이 될 거야.
B 그래. 오늘 밤은 충분히 쉬어야겠다.

기타표현체크

- as much 명사 as possible   가능한 한 ~을 많이
- get a shot   주사를 맞다
- see a doctor   진찰을 받다
- get through sth   (힘든 시기를) 이겨 내다

Mini Dialogues

① feel much better 훨씬 나아지다

A How are you today? Feeling any better?
B I'm feeling much better now. Thanks.

A 오늘 기분은 어때? 좀 나아졌어?
B 지금은 훨씬 좋아졌어. 고마워.

② have a runny nose 콧물이 나오다

A Please have a seat. What are your symptoms?
B I have a runny nose and feel very congested.

A 앉으세요. 증상이 어떻게 되나요?
B 콧물이 나오고 코도 많이 막혀요.

③ take medicine[medication] 약을 복용하다

A It's a relief that I don't have to get surgery.
B Take some medicine and you'll get better soon.

A 수술을 안 받아도 되니 다행이네요.
B 약 좀 드시면 곧 좋아지실 겁니다.

④ get enough rest 충분히 쉬다

A You don't look well. Are you sick or something?
B No. I didn't get enough rest during the weekend.

A 안색이 안 좋네. 어디 아픈 거니?
B 아니. 주말에 충분히 쉬지 못해서.

237

DAY 094

I can't hold my liquor.

저는 술 잘 못 마셔요.

A I should stop here. This is enough for today*.

B No way! Let's **go for another round.**

A I've reached my limit*. I **had one too many.**

B You're kidding. You only had two glasses.

A I **can't hold my liquor.** I'm just a social drinker*.

B Oh, come on*. Let's **have one for the road.**

A 그만 마실래. 오늘 많이 마셨어.
B 말도 안 돼! 2차 하러 가야지.
A 주량이 다 됐어. 너무 많이 마셨어.
B 농담이겠지. 겨우 두 잔 마셨잖아.
A 난 술이 약해. 분위기 맞추는 정도야.
B 왜 그래. 마지막으로 한 잔만 하자.

기타표현체크

- This is enough for today   오늘 많이 마셨어
- social drinker   분위기를 즐기는 사람
- reach one's limit   주량이 다 되다
- Come on   왜 그래, 그러지 마

1 go for another round 2차를 가다

A The night is still young. Let's go for another round.

B Good idea. I know a fancy bar around here.

A 아직 초저녁이야. 우리 2차로 다른 데 가자.
B 좋은 생각이야. 근처에 멋진 술집을 알아.

2 have one too many 너무 많이 마시다

A Are you all right? You're walking so funny.

B I had one too many. It makes me want to puke.

A 괜찮아? 너 이상하게 걷고 있는데.
B 너무 많이 마셨어. 토할 것 같아.

3 can't hold one's liquor 술이 약하다

A You drink like a fish. You can really hold your liquor.

B I'm not what I used to be. As they say, age will tell.

A 술 엄청 마신다. 너 진짜 술이 세구나.
B 예전 같지 않아. 나이는 못 속인다더니.

4 have(drink) one for the road
마지막으로 한 잔 하다

A Let's have one for the road. You don't look fine.

B I think I drank too much on an empty stomach.

A 마지막으로 한 잔만 더 하자. 너 안색이 안 좋아 보여.
B 빈속에 술을 너무 많이 마신 것 같아.

You can say that again.

네 말이 맞아.

A I'm happy to* **get a promotion**. I was lucky.

B Congratulations! You**'re qualified for** the position.

A I didn't expect too much. Things were not good.

B I believe you'll **climb the corporate ladder**.

A Easy for you to say*. It's a dog-eat-dog world*.

B **You can say that again.** It's tough to make a living.*

A 승진해서 기분 좋아. 운이 좋았어.
B 축하해. 넌 그 자리에 자격이 있어.
A 기대를 많이 안 했어. 상황이 안 좋았거든.
B 네가 높은 자리에 갈 거라고 믿어.
A 말은 쉽지. 경쟁이 치열한 세상이야.
B 정말 그래. 먹고 사는 게 쉽지 않아.

기타표현체크

- be happy to + 동사원형 ~하게 되어 기쁘다
- dog-eat-dog world 냉혹한 세계
- Easy for you to say 말이야 쉽지
- make a living 생계를 유지하다

① get a promotion 승진하다

A I finally got a promotion. Let's go for a drink.
B Congratulations! I knew you could pull it off.

A 드디어 승진했어. 술 한잔 하러 가자.
B 축하해! 난 네가 해낼 줄 알았어.

② be qualified for sth ~에 대한 자격이 있다

A Why does he keep failing at job interviews?
B Well, I think he is not qualified for the job.

A 왜 그는 면접에서 계속 떨어지는 거야?
B 그 직업에 자격을 갖추지 못한 것 같아.

③ climb the corporate ladder 출세하다, 승진하다

A Most people try to please your boss but you don't.
B In fact, I'm not into climbing the corporate ladder.

A 대부분 네 상사 비위를 맞추려고 하는데 넌 안 그래.
B 사실은 난 출세하는 것에 별로 흥미가 없어.

④ You can say that again 정말 그래, 동감이야

A What's up with this weather? It's too cold to go out.
B You can say that again. I can't wait for spring to come.

A 날씨가 왜 이래? 너무 추워서 나갈 수가 없어.
B 정말 그래. 빨리 봄이 왔으면 좋겠다.

다음 주어진 우리말을 영어로 말해 보세요.

01 이번 주 토요일에 뭐할 거야?

----

02 휴대폰 없이 어떻게 버텼어?

----

03 약은 먹었지?

----

04 가능한 한 물을 많이 마셔.

----

05 난 술이 약해.

----

06 분위기 맞추는 정도야.

----

07 넌 그 자리에 자격이 있어.

----

08 먹고 사는 게 쉽지 않아.

● 정답 01. What are your plans for this Saturday? 02. How did you get by without the phone? 03. Did you take medicine? 04. Drink as much water as possible. 05. I can't hold my liquor. 06. You're qualified for the position. 07. It's tough to make a living.

DAY
096~100

MP3와 저자 강의를 들어 보세요.

What's eating you?

무슨 고민 있어?

A You look down*. **What's eating you**?

B There was a huge staff reshuffle* yesterday.

A I don't feel good. What happened?

B I got transferred to* the China branch.

A **I'm lost for words. This almost never happens.**

B I'm about to pass out*. I **didn't sign up for this.**

A 우울해 보이네. 무슨 고민 있어?
B 어제 대규모 인사 발령이 있었어.
A 느낌이 안 좋은데. 어떻게 됐어?
B 중국 지사로 발령이 났어.
A 어이없네. 이런 일은 거의 없는데.
B 기절하겠어. 이러려고 입사한 거 아닌데.

기타표현체크

· look down 침울해 보이다
· get transferred to + 부서(지역) ~로 발령 나다
· staff reshuffle 인사 발령
· pass out 기절하다

❶ What's eating you? 무슨 일 있어?

A Why are you so down? What's eating you?

B It's my son. I just have a lot on my mind.

A 왜 이리 시무룩해? 무슨 일 있어?
B 내 아들 때문에. 그냥 생각이 많아.

❷ be lost for words (놀라서) 할 말을 잃다

A I can't believe we met a K-pop star in person.

B When she said, "I love you," I was lost for words.

A 우리가 케이팝 스타를 직접 만나다니 믿을 수가 없어.
B 그녀가 '사랑해요'라고 말했을 때 할 말을 잃었어.

❸ This (almost) never happens
이런 일은 (거의) 절대 없다

A The movie *Parasite* was a huge hit all over the world.

B This almost never happens. I'm proud of my country.

A 영화 〈기생충〉이 전 세계적으로 엄청난 히트를 쳤어.
B 이런 일은 거의 없는데. 우리나라가 자랑스러워.

❹ didn't sign up for this 이러려고 지원(신청)한 거 아니다

A What the heck are you doing? Do as you're told.

B With all due respect, I didn't sign up for this.

A 도대체 뭐 하는 거야? 시키는 대로 좀 해.
B 죄송하지만, 이런 일 하려고 지원한 거 아니에요.

DAY 097

Don't hold anything back.

숨기지 말고 말해 봐.

🎧 Day 097

MP3 강의 듣기

A Can I **sleep over at Daniel's place*** tonight?

B What's up? **Don't hold anything back.**

A We're **having a year-end party** overnight*.

B I'm terrible with names. What was his name again?

A Daniel. His parents went on a trip* yesterday.

B OK. I'll catch a late-night movie* with your dad.

A 오늘 다니엘 집에서 자도 돼요?

B 무슨 일인데? 숨기지 말고 말해 봐.

A 밤새도록 송년파티를 할 거예요.

B 내가 이름을 잘 못 외워. 친구 이름이 뭐라고?

A 다니엘이요. 어제 부모님이 여행 가셨어요.

B 알았어. 네 아빠하고 심야 영화나 봐야겠다.

기타표현체크

- sb's place ~의 집
- go on a trip 여행을 가다
- overnight 밤새도록
- catch a late-night movie 심야 영화를 보다

① sleep over at one's place ~의 집에서 자다

A I'll have a party. Can you sleep over at my place?
B That'll be fun. You got the go-ahead from your mom?

A 파티를 할 건데. 우리 집에서 자고 갈래?
B 재미있겠다. 너희 엄마한테 허락받았어?

---

② don't hold anything back 아무것도 숨기지 않다

A I feel like you didn't tell me the truth.
B Please believe me. I didn't hold anything back.

A 네가 나에게 거짓말했다는 느낌이 드는데.
B 내 말을 믿어줘. 아무것도 숨기지 않았어.

---

③ have a year-end party 송년파티를 하다

A I have a lot of get-togethers over the holiday season.
B We should have a year-end party before the year ends.

A 연휴 기간에는 모임이 정말 많아.
B 우리도 해가 끝나기 전에 송년회를 해야겠다.

---

④ be terrible with sth ~에 서투르다

A I guess this navigation system is all messed up.
B What am I going to do? I'm terrible with directions.

A 이 내비게이션은 완전 맛이 간 것 같아.
B 어떻게 하지? 나 진짜 길눈 어두운데.

🎧 Day 098

MP3 강의 듣기

I'll check if I can clear up my schedule.

일정을 비울 수 있는지 볼게.

A Are you **taking a vacation** for Christmas?

B Yes, I'm going to **join a group tour** to China.

A Good for you! I want to **kick back and relax**.

B I need some company*. Will you join me?

A Sounds tempting*. I'll see if I can **clear up my schedule.**

B You won't be sorry*. You have my word*.

A 크리스마스 때 휴가 갈 거야?
B 응, 중국으로 단체 여행을 갈 거야.
A 좋겠다. 나도 좀 푹 쉬고 싶은데.
B 일행이 필요한데. 같이 갈래?
A 솔깃한데. 일정을 비울 수 있는지 볼게.
B 후회하지 않을 거야. 약속해.

기타표현체크

- company 일행
- You won't be sorry 후회하지 않을 거야
- Sounds tempting 끌리는데
- You have my word 약속해, 믿어도 돼

❶ take a vacation 휴가를 내다

A When are you gonna take a vacation this summer?
B I'm not sure. I need to plan my schedule.

A 올 여름 휴가를 언제 낼 예정인가요?
B 잘 모르겠어요. 일정을 짜 봐야죠.

❷ join a group tour (to 목적지) 단체 여행을 가다

A My family will join a group tour with a tour guide.
B It really helps when you're not familiar with the area.

A 우리 가족은 가이드와 단체 여행을 갈 거야.
B 그 지역에 대해 잘 모를 때는 큰 도움이 되지.

❸ kick back and relax 긴장을 풀고 푹 쉬다

A Is there a good place to kick back and relax?
B I know a beach cottage with a swimming pool.

A 긴장을 풀고 편히 쉴 만한 곳 있을까?
B 수영장 있는 비치 펜션을 알고 있어.

❹ clear up one's schedule 스케줄(일정)을 비우다

A Can you clear up your morning schedule tomorrow?
B I'm afraid I can't give you an answer right now.

A 내일 오전 스케줄 좀 비워 줄 수 있어?
B 미안한데 지금 바로 대답해 줄 수가 없어.

MP3 강의 듣기

DAY 099

I'm having mixed feelings tonight.

오늘 밤엔 만감이 교차한다.

A Time seems to move faster* every year.

B We've **had a lot of ups and downs** this year.

A Right. I'm **having mixed feelings** tonight.

B I **feel like** something is missing* at the end of the year.

A It's a bitter-sweet feeling*. Let's make a toast*.

B **Here's to** our friendship and future.

A 매년 시간이 더 빨리 가는 것 같아.
B 올해도 정말 우여곡절이 많았지.
A 그래. 오늘 밤엔 만감이 교차한다.
B 연말에는 뭔가 허전한 기분이 들어.
A 시원섭섭한 감정이지. 건배하자.
B (건배) 우리의 우정과 미래를 위하여!

기타표현체크

- move[go by] fast　(시간이) 빨리 지나가다
- sth is missing　뭔가 허전하다
- bitter-sweet feeling　시원섭섭한 감정
- make a toast (to sth)　(~를 위해) 건배 제의하다

 **Mini Dialogues**

① have a lot of ups and downs 우여곡절을 겪다

A My CEO had a lot of ups and downs in life.

B He started out poor and dropped out of college.

A 우리 CEO는 수많은 우여곡절을 경험하셨어.

B 가난하게 시작하셨고 대학교도 중퇴하셨지.

② have mixed feelings (about sth)
여러 가지 감정이 들다

A I appreciate your commitment. I hope things will work out.

B I can't believe I'm retiring. I have mixed feelings about it.

A 그동안 수고 많으셨습니다. 일이 잘 되길 바랄게요.

B 은퇴를 하다니 믿기지 않아요. 만감이 교차합니다.

③ feel like 주어+동사 ~와 같은 기분이 들다

A I feel like I had a dream about you last night.

B Thank you. I think you love me so much.

A 어젯밤에 네 꿈을 꾼 것 같아.

B 고마워. 날 많이 사랑하는 것 같네.

④ Here is to sth ~을 위하여 건배!

A I'd like to propose a toast to the bride and groom.

B Here is to happiness for our just married couple.

A 신랑과 신부를 위해 건배를 제의합니다.

B 이제 갓 결혼한 부부의 행복을 위하여!

DAY 100

I hope you make it big next year.

내년에 대박 나길 바라.

A Happy new year! I hope you **make it big** next year.

B My family is climbing a mountain* to see the sunrise*.

A I guess you will **make a wish** for the new year.

B It's sort of a ritual* at the beginning of the year*.

A My mother and I will go to **get our fortunes told.**

B Really? You should **take** it **with a grain of salt**.

A 새해 복 많이 받아. 내년에 대박 나길 바라.
B 우리 가족은 일출 보러 등산할 거야.
A 신년 소원도 빌겠구나.
B 연초에 하는 의례 같은 거잖아.
A 난 엄마하고 운세 보러 가려고.
B 정말? 적당히 걸러서 들어.

기타표현체크

- climb a mountain   등산을 하다
- ritual   의식, 의례
- see the sunrise   일출을 보다
- at the beginning of the year   연초에

① make it big 크게 성공하다

A I was asked to be on TV next week.

B Great! I knew you would make it big someday.

A 다음주에 TV 출연 제의를 받았어.
B 대단해! 언젠가 네가 성공할거라는 거 알았어.

② make a wish (for sth) ~을 위해 소원을 빌다

A Come here. Make a wish and blow out the candles.

B What a surprise! I never imagined you guys doing this.

A 이리 와 봐. 소원 빌고 촛불을 꺼.
B 깜짝이야! 너희가 이럴 거라곤 생각도 못했어.

③ get one's fortunes told 운세를 보다

A Let's go get our fortunes told. I know a good place.

B I don't believe in it. I think that's a waste of time.

A 운세 보러 가자. 내가 잘 보는 데 알아.
B 난 그런 거 안 믿어. 시간 낭비인 것 같아.

④ take sth with a grain of salt 걸러서 받아들이다

A I don't like him because he always brags a lot.

B You should take what he says with a grain of salt.

A 걔는 늘 허풍이 심해서 싫어.
B 그가 하는 말은 걸러서 들어야 해.

다음 주어진 우리말을 영어로 말해 보세요.

01 우울해 보이네.

----

02 무슨 고민 있어?

----

03 숨기지 말고 말해 봐.

----

04 내가 이름을 잘 못 외워.

----

05 나도 좀 푹 쉬고 싶은데.

----

06 약속해.

----

07 우리 건배하자.

----

08 내년에 대박 나길 바라.

●정답 01. You look down. 02. What's eating you? 03. Don't hold anything back. 04. I'm terrible with names. 05. I want to kick back and relax. 06. You have my word. 07. Let's make a toast. 08. I hope you make it big next year.

MEMO